THIS IS YOUR **PASSBOOK®** FOR ...

COMPUTER PROGRAMMER ANALYST TRAINEE

NATIONAL LEARNING CORPORATION®
passbooks.com

PASSBOOK® SERIES

THE *PASSBOOK® SERIES* has been created to prepare applicants and candidates for the ultimate academic battlefield – the examination room.

At some time in our lives, each and every one of us may be required to take an examination – for validation, matriculation, admission, qualification, registration, certification, or licensure.

Based on the assumption that every applicant or candidate has met the basic formal educational standards, has taken the required number of courses, and read the necessary texts, the *PASSBOOK® SERIES* furnishes the one special preparation which may assure passing with confidence, instead of failing with insecurity. Examination questions – together with answers – are furnished as the basic vehicle for study so that the mysteries of the examination and its compounding difficulties may be eliminated or diminished by a sure method.

This book is meant to help you pass your examination provided that you qualify and are serious in your objective.

The entire field is reviewed through the huge store of content information which is succinctly presented through a provocative and challenging approach – the question-and-answer method.

A climate of success is established by furnishing the correct answers at the end of each test.

You soon learn to recognize types of questions, forms of questions, and patterns of questioning. You may even begin to anticipate expected outcomes.

You perceive that many questions are repeated or adapted so that you can gain acute insights, which may enable you to score many sure points.

You learn how to confront new questions, or types of questions, and to attack them confidently and work out the correct answers.

You note objectives and emphases, and recognize pitfalls and dangers, so that you may make positive educational adjustments.

Moreover, you are kept fully informed in relation to new concepts, methods, practices, and directions in the field.

You discover that you arre actually taking the examination all the time: you are preparing for the examination by "taking" an examination, not by reading extraneous and/or supererogatory textbooks.

In short, this PASSBOOK®, used directedly, should be an important factor in helping you to pass your test.

COMPUTER PROGRAMMER ANALYST TRAINEE

DUTIES AND RESPONSIBILITIES
Under direct or immediate supervision, with little latitude for independent or unreviewed action or decision, is trained in and performs beginning level professional work for the purpose of acquiring knowledge, skill and competence in the development of programs for use in the operations of an electronic digital computer system; performs related work.

EXAMPLES OF TYPICAL TASKS
Receives a course of training, and, under close supervision, performs the following tasks: Assists in the review and analysis of detailed computer systems specifications; assists in the preparation of program instructions; assists in the preparation of block diagrams; codes program instructions; assists in the preparation of test data and in testing and debugging programs; assists in the preparation of the documentation of the program for the computer operators, and set-up persons.

TESTS
The written test will be of the multiple-choice type and may include questions on logical reasoning including figure analogies and flowcharts, reading comprehension, arithmetic skills including number sequences, interpersonal relations, and other related areas.

PROMOTION OPPORTUNITIES
Employees in the title of Computer Programmer Analyst are accorded promotion opportunities, when eligible, to the title of Computer Associate (Applications Programming) or Computer Associate (Systems Programming).

HOW TO TAKE A TEST

I. YOU MUST PASS AN EXAMINATION

A. *WHAT EVERY CANDIDATE SHOULD KNOW*

Examination applicants often ask us for help in preparing for the written test. What can I study in advance? What kinds of questions will be asked? How will the test be given? How will the papers be graded?

As an applicant for a civil service examination, you may be wondering about some of these things. Our purpose here is to suggest effective methods of advance study and to describe civil service examinations.

Your chances for success on this examination can be increased if you know how to prepare. Those "pre-examination jitters" can be reduced if you know what to expect. You can even experience an adventure in good citizenship if you know why civil service exams are given.

B. *WHY ARE CIVIL SERVICE EXAMINATIONS GIVEN?*

Civil service examinations are important to you in two ways. As a citizen, you want public jobs filled by employees who know how to do their work. As a job seeker, you want a fair chance to compete for that job on an equal footing with other candidates. The best-known means of accomplishing this two-fold goal is the competitive examination.

Exams are widely publicized throughout the nation. They may be administered for jobs in federal, state, city, municipal, town or village governments or agencies.

Any citizen may apply, with some limitations, such as the age or residence of applicants. Your experience and education may be reviewed to see whether you meet the requirements for the particular examination. When these requirements exist, they are reasonable and applied consistently to all applicants. Thus, a competitive examination may cause you some uneasiness now, but it is your privilege and safeguard.

C. *HOW ARE CIVIL SERVICE EXAMS DEVELOPED?*

Examinations are carefully written by trained technicians who are specialists in the field known as "psychological measurement," in consultation with recognized authorities in the field of work that the test will cover. These experts recommend the subject matter areas or skills to be tested; only those knowledges or skills important to your success on the job are included. The most reliable books and source materials available are used as references. Together, the experts and technicians judge the difficulty level of the questions.

Test technicians know how to phrase questions so that the problem is clearly stated. Their ethics do not permit "trick" or "catch" questions. Questions may have been tried out on sample groups, or subjected to statistical analysis, to determine their usefulness.

Written tests are often used in combination with performance tests, ratings of training and experience, and oral interviews. All of these measures combine to form the best-known means of finding the right person for the right job.

II. HOW TO PASS THE WRITTEN TEST

A. NATURE OF THE EXAMINATION

To prepare intelligently for civil service examinations, you should know how they differ from school examinations you have taken. In school you were assigned certain definite pages to read or subjects to cover. The examination questions were quite detailed and usually emphasized memory. Civil service exams, on the other hand, try to discover your present ability to perform the duties of a position, plus your potentiality to learn these duties. In other words, a civil service exam attempts to predict how successful you will be. Questions cover such a broad area that they cannot be as minute and detailed as school exam questions.

In the public service similar kinds of work, or positions, are grouped together in one "class." This process is known as *position-classification*. All the positions in a class are paid according to the salary range for that class. One class title covers all of these positions, and they are all tested by the same examination.

B. FOUR BASIC STEPS

1) Study the announcement

How, then, can you know what subjects to study? Our best answer is: "Learn as much as possible about the class of positions for which you've applied." The exam will test the knowledge, skills and abilities needed to do the work.

Your most valuable source of information about the position you want is the official exam announcement. This announcement lists the training and experience qualifications. Check these standards and apply only if you come reasonably close to meeting them.

The brief description of the position in the examination announcement offers some clues to the subjects which will be tested. Think about the job itself. Review the duties in your mind. Can you perform them, or are there some in which you are rusty? Fill in the blank spots in your preparation.

Many jurisdictions preview the written test in the exam announcement by including a section called "Knowledge and Abilities Required," "Scope of the Examination," or some similar heading. Here you will find out specifically what fields will be tested.

2) Review your own background

Once you learn in general what the position is all about, and what you need to know to do the work, ask yourself which subjects you already know fairly well and which need improvement. You may wonder whether to concentrate on improving your strong areas or on building some background in your fields of weakness. When the announcement has specified "some knowledge" or "considerable knowledge," or has used adjectives like "beginning principles of…" or "advanced … methods," you can get a clue as to the number and difficulty of questions to be asked in any given field. More questions, and hence broader coverage, would be included for those subjects which are more important in the work. Now weigh your strengths and weaknesses against the job requirements and prepare accordingly.

3) Determine the level of the position

Another way to tell how intensively you should prepare is to understand the level of the job for which you are applying. Is it the entering level? In other words, is this the position in which beginners in a field of work are hired? Or is it an intermediate or advanced level? Sometimes this is indicated by such words as "Junior" or "Senior" in the class title. Other jurisdictions use Roman numerals to designate the level – Clerk I, Clerk II, for example. The word "Supervisor" sometimes appears in the title. If the level is not indicated by the title, check the description of duties. Will you be working under very close supervision, or will you have responsibility for independent decisions in this work?

4) Choose appropriate study materials

Now that you know the subjects to be examined and the relative amount of each subject to be covered, you can choose suitable study materials. For beginning level jobs, or even advanced ones, if you have a pronounced weakness in some aspect of your training, read a modern, standard textbook in that field. Be sure it is up to date and has general coverage. Such books are normally available at your library, and the librarian will be glad to help you locate one. For entry-level positions, questions of appropriate difficulty are chosen – neither highly advanced questions, nor those too simple. Such questions require careful thought but not advanced training.

If the position for which you are applying is technical or advanced, you will read more advanced, specialized material. If you are already familiar with the basic principles of your field, elementary textbooks would waste your time. Concentrate on advanced textbooks and technical periodicals. Think through the concepts and review difficult problems in your field.

These are all general sources. You can get more ideas on your own initiative, following these leads. For example, training manuals and publications of the government agency which employs workers in your field can be useful, particularly for technical and professional positions. A letter or visit to the government department involved may result in more specific study suggestions, and certainly will provide you with a more definite idea of the exact nature of the position you are seeking.

III. KINDS OF TESTS

Tests are used for purposes other than measuring knowledge and ability to perform specified duties. For some positions, it is equally important to test ability to make adjustments to new situations or to profit from training. In others, basic mental abilities not dependent on information are essential. Questions which test these things may not appear as pertinent to the duties of the position as those which test for knowledge and information. Yet they are often highly important parts of a fair examination. For very general questions, it is almost impossible to help you direct your study efforts. What we can do is to point out some of the more common of these general abilities needed in public service positions and describe some typical questions.

1) General information

Broad, general information has been found useful for predicting job success in some kinds of work. This is tested in a variety of ways, from vocabulary lists to questions about current events. Basic background in some field of work, such as sociology or economics, may be sampled in a group of questions. Often these are principles which have become familiar to most persons through exposure rather than through formal training. It is difficult to advise you how to study for these questions; being alert to the world around you is our best suggestion.

2) Verbal ability

An example of an ability needed in many positions is verbal or language ability. Verbal ability is, in brief, the ability to use and understand words. Vocabulary and grammar tests are typical measures of this ability. Reading comprehension or paragraph interpretation questions are common in many kinds of civil service tests. You are given a paragraph of written material and asked to find its central meaning.

3) Numerical ability

Number skills can be tested by the familiar arithmetic problem, by checking paired lists of numbers to see which are alike and which are different, or by interpreting charts and graphs. In the latter test, a graph may be printed in the test booklet which you are asked to use as the basis for answering questions.

4) Observation

A popular test for law-enforcement positions is the observation test. A picture is shown to you for several minutes, then taken away. Questions about the picture test your ability to observe both details and larger elements.

5) Following directions

In many positions in the public service, the employee must be able to carry out written instructions dependably and accurately. You may be given a chart with several columns, each column listing a variety of information. The questions require you to carry out directions involving the information given in the chart.

6) Skills and aptitudes

Performance tests effectively measure some manual skills and aptitudes. When the skill is one in which you are trained, such as typing or shorthand, you can practice. These tests are often very much like those given in business school or high school courses. For many of the other skills and aptitudes, however, no short-time preparation can be made. Skills and abilities natural to you or that you have developed throughout your lifetime are being tested.

Many of the general questions just described provide all the data needed to answer the questions and ask you to use your reasoning ability to find the answers. Your best preparation for these tests, as well as for tests of facts and ideas, is to be at your physical and mental best. You, no doubt, have your own methods of getting into an exam-taking mood and keeping "in shape." The next section lists some ideas on this subject.

IV. KINDS OF QUESTIONS

Only rarely is the "essay" question, which you answer in narrative form, used in civil service tests. Civil service tests are usually of the short-answer type. Full instructions for answering these questions will be given to you at the examination. But in case this is your first experience with short-answer questions and separate answer sheets, here is what you need to know:

1) Multiple-choice Questions

Most popular of the short-answer questions is the "multiple choice" or "best answer" question. It can be used, for example, to test for factual knowledge, ability to solve problems or judgment in meeting situations found at work.

A multiple-choice question is normally one of three types—

- It can begin with an incomplete statement followed by several possible endings. You are to find the one ending which *best* completes the statement, although some of the others may not be entirely wrong.
- It can also be a complete statement in the form of a question which is answered by choosing one of the statements listed.
- It can be in the form of a problem – again you select the best answer.

Here is an example of a multiple-choice question with a discussion which should give you some clues as to the method for choosing the right answer:

When an employee has a complaint about his assignment, the action which will *best* help him overcome his difficulty is to
- A. discuss his difficulty with his coworkers
- B. take the problem to the head of the organization
- C. take the problem to the person who gave him the assignment
- D. say nothing to anyone about his complaint

In answering this question, you should study each of the choices to find which is best. Consider choice "A" – Certainly an employee may discuss his complaint with fellow employees, but no change or improvement can result, and the complaint remains unresolved. Choice "B" is a poor choice since the head of the organization probably does not know what assignment you have been given, and taking your problem to him is known as "going over the head" of the supervisor. The supervisor, or person who made the assignment, is the person who can clarify it or correct any injustice. Choice "C" is, therefore, correct. To say nothing, as in choice "D," is unwise. Supervisors have and interest in knowing the problems employees are facing, and the employee is seeking a solution to his problem.

2) True/False Questions

The "true/false" or "right/wrong" form of question is sometimes used. Here a complete statement is given. Your job is to decide whether the statement is right or wrong.

SAMPLE: A roaming cell-phone call to a nearby city costs less than a non-roaming call to a distant city.

This statement is wrong, or false, since roaming calls are more expensive.
This is not a complete list of all possible question forms, although most of the others are variations of these common types. You will always get complete directions for

answering questions. Be sure you understand *how* to mark your answers – ask questions until you do.

V. RECORDING YOUR ANSWERS

Computer terminals are used more and more today for many different kinds of exams.

For an examination with very few applicants, you may be told to record your answers in the test booklet itself. Separate answer sheets are much more common. If this separate answer sheet is to be scored by machine – and this is often the case – it is highly important that you mark your answers correctly in order to get credit.

An electronic scoring machine is often used in civil service offices because of the speed with which papers can be scored. Machine-scored answer sheets must be marked with a pencil, which will be given to you. This pencil has a high graphite content which responds to the electronic scoring machine. As a matter of fact, stray dots may register as answers, so do not let your pencil rest on the answer sheet while you are pondering the correct answer. Also, if your pencil lead breaks or is otherwise defective, ask for another.

Since the answer sheet will be dropped in a slot in the scoring machine, be careful not to bend the corners or get the paper crumpled.

The answer sheet normally has five vertical columns of numbers, with 30 numbers to a column. These numbers correspond to the question numbers in your test booklet. After each number, going across the page are four or five pairs of dotted lines. These short dotted lines have small letters or numbers above them. The first two pairs may also have a "T" or "F" above the letters. This indicates that the first two pairs only are to be used if the questions are of the true-false type. If the questions are multiple choice, disregard the "T" and "F" and pay attention only to the small letters or numbers.

Answer your questions in the manner of the sample that follows:

32. The largest city in the United States is
    A. Washington, D.C.
    B. New York City
    C. Chicago
    D. Detroit
    E. San Francisco

1) Choose the answer you think is best. (New York City is the largest, so "B" is correct.)
2) Find the row of dotted lines numbered the same as the question you are answering. (Find row number 32)
3) Find the pair of dotted lines corresponding to the answer. (Find the pair of lines under the mark "B.")
4) Make a solid black mark between the dotted lines.

VI. BEFORE THE TEST

Common sense will help you find procedures to follow to get ready for an examination. Too many of us, however, overlook these sensible measures. Indeed, nervousness and fatigue have been found to be the most serious reasons why applicants fail to do their best on civil service tests. Here is a list of reminders:

- Begin your preparation early – Don't wait until the last minute to go scurrying around for books and materials or to find out what the position is all about.
- Prepare continuously – An hour a night for a week is better than an all-night cram session. This has been definitely established. What is more, a night a week for a month will return better dividends than crowding your study into a shorter period of time.
- Locate the place of the exam – You have been sent a notice telling you when and where to report for the examination. If the location is in a different town or otherwise unfamiliar to you, it would be well to inquire the best route and learn something about the building.
- Relax the night before the test – Allow your mind to rest. Do not study at all that night. Plan some mild recreation or diversion; then go to bed early and get a good night's sleep.
- Get up early enough to make a leisurely trip to the place for the test – This way unforeseen events, traffic snarls, unfamiliar buildings, etc. will not upset you.
- Dress comfortably – A written test is not a fashion show. You will be known by number and not by name, so wear something comfortable.
- Leave excess paraphernalia at home – Shopping bags and odd bundles will get in your way. You need bring only the items mentioned in the official notice you received; usually everything you need is provided. Do not bring reference books to the exam. They will only confuse those last minutes and be taken away from you when in the test room.
- Arrive somewhat ahead of time – If because of transportation schedules you must get there very early, bring a newspaper or magazine to take your mind off yourself while waiting.
- Locate the examination room – When you have found the proper room, you will be directed to the seat or part of the room where you will sit. Sometimes you are given a sheet of instructions to read while you are waiting. Do not fill out any forms until you are told to do so; just read them and be prepared.
- Relax and prepare to listen to the instructions
- If you have any physical problem that may keep you from doing your best, be sure to tell the test administrator. If you are sick or in poor health, you really cannot do your best on the exam. You can come back and take the test some other time.

VII. AT THE TEST

The day of the test is here and you have the test booklet in your hand. The temptation to get going is very strong. Caution! There is more to success than knowing the right answers. You must know how to identify your papers and understand variations in the type of short-answer question used in this particular examination. Follow these suggestions for maximum results from your efforts:

1) Cooperate with the monitor

The test administrator has a duty to create a situation in which you can be as much at ease as possible. He will give instructions, tell you when to begin, check to see that you are marking your answer sheet correctly, and so on. He is not there to guard you, although he will see that your competitors do not take unfair advantage. He wants to help you do your best.

2) Listen to all instructions

Don't jump the gun! Wait until you understand all directions. In most civil service tests you get more time than you need to answer the questions. So don't be in a hurry. Read each word of instructions until you clearly understand the meaning. Study the examples, listen to all announcements and follow directions. Ask questions if you do not understand what to do.

3) Identify your papers

Civil service exams are usually identified by number only. You will be assigned a number; you must not put your name on your test papers. Be sure to copy your number correctly. Since more than one exam may be given, copy your exact examination title.

4) Plan your time

Unless you are told that a test is a "speed" or "rate of work" test, speed itself is usually not important. Time enough to answer all the questions will be provided, but this does not mean that you have all day. An overall time limit has been set. Divide the total time (in minutes) by the number of questions to determine the approximate time you have for each question.

5) Do not linger over difficult questions

If you come across a difficult question, mark it with a paper clip (useful to have along) and come back to it when you have been through the booklet. One caution if you do this – be sure to skip a number on your answer sheet as well. Check often to be sure that you have not lost your place and that you are marking in the row numbered the same as the question you are answering.

6) Read the questions

Be sure you know what the question asks! Many capable people are unsuccessful because they failed to *read* the questions correctly.

7) Answer all questions

Unless you have been instructed that a penalty will be deducted for incorrect answers, it is better to guess than to omit a question.

8) Speed tests

It is often better NOT to guess on speed tests. It has been found that on timed tests people are tempted to spend the last few seconds before time is called in marking answers at random – without even reading them – in the hope of picking up a few extra points. To discourage this practice, the instructions may warn you that your score will be "corrected" for guessing. That is, a penalty will be applied. The incorrect answers will be deducted from the correct ones, or some other penalty formula will be used.

9) Review your answers

If you finish before time is called, go back to the questions you guessed or omitted to give them further thought. Review other answers if you have time.

10) Return your test materials

If you are ready to leave before others have finished or time is called, take ALL your materials to the monitor and leave quietly. Never take any test material with you. The monitor can discover whose papers are not complete, and taking a test booklet may be grounds for disqualification.

VIII. EXAMINATION TECHNIQUES

1) Read the general instructions carefully. These are usually printed on the first page of the exam booklet. As a rule, these instructions refer to the timing of the examination; the fact that you should not start work until the signal and must stop work at a signal, etc. If there are any *special* instructions, such as a choice of questions to be answered, make sure that you note this instruction carefully.

2) When you are ready to start work on the examination, that is as soon as the signal has been given, read the instructions to each question booklet, underline any key words or phrases, such as *least, best, outline, describe* and the like. In this way you will tend to answer as requested rather than discover on reviewing your paper that you *listed without describing*, that you selected the *worst* choice rather than the *best* choice, etc.

3) If the examination is of the objective or multiple-choice type – that is, each question will also give a series of possible answers: A, B, C or D, and you are called upon to select the best answer and write the letter next to that answer on your answer paper – it is advisable to start answering each question in turn. There may be anywhere from 50 to 100 such questions in the three or four hours allotted and you can see how much time would be taken if you read through all the questions before beginning to answer any. Furthermore, if you come across a question or group of questions which you know would be difficult to answer, it would undoubtedly affect your handling of all the other questions.

4) If the examination is of the essay type and contains but a few questions, it is a moot point as to whether you should read all the questions before starting to answer any one. Of course, if you are given a choice – say five out of seven and the like – then it is essential to read all the questions so you can eliminate the two that are most difficult. If, however, you are asked to answer all the questions, there may be danger in trying to answer the easiest one first because you may find that you will spend too much time on it. The best technique is to answer the first question, then proceed to the second, etc.

5) Time your answers. Before the exam begins, write down the time it started, then add the time allowed for the examination and write down the time it must be completed, then divide the time available somewhat as follows:

- If 3-1/2 hours are allowed, that would be 210 minutes. If you have 80 objective-type questions, that would be an average of 2-1/2 minutes per question. Allow yourself no more than 2 minutes per question, or a total of 160 minutes, which will permit about 50 minutes to review.
- If for the time allotment of 210 minutes there are 7 essay questions to answer, that would average about 30 minutes a question. Give yourself only 25 minutes per question so that you have about 35 minutes to review.

6) The most important instruction is to *read each question* and make sure you know what is wanted. The second most important instruction is to *time yourself properly* so that you answer every question. The third most important instruction is to *answer every question.* Guess if you have to but include something for each question. Remember that you will receive no credit for a blank and will probably receive some credit if you write something in answer to an essay question. If you guess a letter – say "B" for a multiple-choice question – you may have guessed right. If you leave a blank as an answer to a multiple-choice question, the examiners may respect your feelings but it will not add a point to your score. Some exams may penalize you for wrong answers, so in such cases *only*, you may not want to guess unless you have some basis for your answer.

7) Suggestions
   a. Objective-type questions
      1. Examine the question booklet for proper sequence of pages and questions
      2. Read all instructions carefully
      3. Skip any question which seems too difficult; return to it after all other questions have been answered
      4. Apportion your time properly; do not spend too much time on any single question or group of questions
      5. Note and underline key words – *all, most, fewest, least, best, worst, same, opposite,* etc.
      6. Pay particular attention to negatives
      7. Note unusual option, e.g., unduly long, short, complex, different or similar in content to the body of the question
      8. Observe the use of "hedging" words – *probably, may, most likely,* etc.
      9. Make sure that your answer is put next to the same number as the question
      10. Do not second-guess unless you have good reason to believe the second answer is definitely more correct
      11. Cross out original answer if you decide another answer is more accurate; do not erase until you are ready to hand your paper in
      12. Answer all questions; guess unless instructed otherwise
      13. Leave time for review

   b. Essay questions
      1. Read each question carefully
      2. Determine exactly what is wanted. Underline key words or phrases.
      3. Decide on outline or paragraph answer

4. Include many different points and elements unless asked to develop any one or two points or elements
5. Show impartiality by giving pros and cons unless directed to select one side only
6. Make and write down any assumptions you find necessary to answer the questions
7. Watch your English, grammar, punctuation and choice of words
8. Time your answers; don't crowd material

8) Answering the essay question

Most essay questions can be answered by framing the specific response around several key words or ideas. Here are a few such key words or ideas:

M's: manpower, materials, methods, money, management
P's: purpose, program, policy, plan, procedure, practice, problems, pitfalls, personnel, public relations
   a. Six basic steps in handling problems:
      1. Preliminary plan and background development
      2. Collect information, data and facts
      3. Analyze and interpret information, data and facts
      4. Analyze and develop solutions as well as make recommendations
      5. Prepare report and sell recommendations
      6. Install recommendations and follow up effectiveness

   b. Pitfalls to avoid
      1. *Taking things for granted* – A statement of the situation does not necessarily imply that each of the elements is necessarily true; for example, a complaint may be invalid and biased so that all that can be taken for granted is that a complaint has been registered
      2. *Considering only one side of a situation* – Wherever possible, indicate several alternatives and then point out the reasons you selected the best one
      3. *Failing to indicate follow up* – Whenever your answer indicates action on your part, make certain that you will take proper follow-up action to see how successful your recommendations, procedures or actions turn out to be
      4. *Taking too long in answering any single question* – Remember to time your answers properly

IX. AFTER THE TEST

Scoring procedures differ in detail among civil service jurisdictions although the general principles are the same. Whether the papers are hand-scored or graded by machine we have described, they are nearly always graded by number. That is, the person who marks the paper knows only the number – never the name – of the applicant. Not until all the papers have been graded will they be matched with names. If other tests, such as training and experience or oral interview ratings have been given, scores will be combined. Different parts of the examination usually have different weights. For example, the written test might count 60 percent of the final grade, and a rating of training and experience 40 percent. In many jurisdictions, veterans will have a certain number of points added to their grades.

After the final grade has been determined, the names are placed in grade order and an eligible list is established. There are various methods for resolving ties between those who get the same final grade – probably the most common is to place first the name of the person whose application was received first. Job offers are made from the eligible list in the order the names appear on it. You will be notified of your grade and your rank as soon as all these computations have been made. This will be done as rapidly as possible.

People who are found to meet the requirements in the announcement are called "eligibles." Their names are put on a list of eligible candidates. An eligible's chances of getting a job depend on how high he stands on this list and how fast agencies are filling jobs from the list.

When a job is to be filled from a list of eligibles, the agency asks for the names of people on the list of eligibles for that job. When the civil service commission receives this request, it sends to the agency the names of the three people highest on this list. Or, if the job to be filled has specialized requirements, the office sends the agency the names of the top three persons who meet these requirements from the general list.

The appointing officer makes a choice from among the three people whose names were sent to him. If the selected person accepts the appointment, the names of the others are put back on the list to be considered for future openings.

That is the rule in hiring from all kinds of eligible lists, whether they are for typist, carpenter, chemist, or something else. For every vacancy, the appointing officer has his choice of any one of the top three eligibles on the list. This explains why the person whose name is on top of the list sometimes does not get an appointment when some of the persons lower on the list do. If the appointing officer chooses the second or third eligible, the No. 1 eligible does not get a job at once, but stays on the list until he is appointed or the list is terminated.

X. HOW TO PASS THE INTERVIEW TEST

The examination for which you applied requires an oral interview test. You have already taken the written test and you are now being called for the interview test – the final part of the formal examination.

You may think that it is not possible to prepare for an interview test and that there are no procedures to follow during an interview. Our purpose is to point out some things you can do in advance that will help you and some good rules to follow and pitfalls to avoid while you are being interviewed.

What is an interview supposed to test?
The written examination is designed to test the technical knowledge and competence of the candidate; the oral is designed to evaluate intangible qualities, not readily measured otherwise, and to establish a list showing the relative fitness of each candidate – as measured against his competitors – for the position sought. Scoring is not on the basis of "right" and "wrong," but on a sliding scale of values ranging from "not passable" to "outstanding." As a matter of fact, it is possible to achieve a relatively low score without a single "incorrect" answer because of evident weakness in the qualities being measured.

Occasionally, an examination may consist entirely of an oral test – either an individual or a group oral. In such cases, information is sought concerning the technical knowledges and abilities of the candidate, since there has been no written examination for this purpose. More commonly, however, an oral test is used to supplement a written examination.

Who conducts interviews?

The composition of oral boards varies among different jurisdictions. In nearly all, a representative of the personnel department serves as chairman. One of the members of the board may be a representative of the department in which the candidate would work. In some cases, "outside experts" are used, and, frequently, a businessman or some other representative of the general public is asked to serve. Labor and management or other special groups may be represented. The aim is to secure the services of experts in the appropriate field.

However the board is composed, it is a good idea (and not at all improper or unethical) to ascertain in advance of the interview who the members are and what groups they represent. When you are introduced to them, you will have some idea of their backgrounds and interests, and at least you will not stutter and stammer over their names.

What should be done before the interview?

While knowledge about the board members is useful and takes some of the surprise element out of the interview, there is other preparation which is more substantive. It *is* possible to prepare for an oral interview – in several ways:

1) Keep a copy of your application and review it carefully before the interview

This may be the only document before the oral board, and the starting point of the interview. Know what education and experience you have listed there, and the sequence and dates of all of it. Sometimes the board will ask you to review the highlights of your experience for them; you should not have to hem and haw doing it.

2) Study the class specification and the examination announcement

Usually, the oral board has one or both of these to guide them. The qualities, characteristics or knowledges required by the position sought are stated in these documents. They offer valuable clues as to the nature of the oral interview. For example, if the job involves supervisory responsibilities, the announcement will usually indicate that knowledge of modern supervisory methods and the qualifications of the candidate as a supervisor will be tested. If so, you can expect such questions, frequently in the form of a hypothetical situation which you are expected to solve. NEVER go into an oral without knowledge of the duties and responsibilities of the job you seek.

3) Think through each qualification required

Try to visualize the kind of questions you would ask if you were a board member. How well could you answer them? Try especially to appraise your own knowledge and background in each area, *measured against the job sought*, and identify any areas in which you are weak. Be critical and realistic – do not flatter yourself.

4) Do some general reading in areas in which you feel you may be weak

For example, if the job involves supervision and your past experience has NOT, some general reading in supervisory methods and practices, particularly in the field of human relations, might be useful. Do NOT study agency procedures or detailed manuals. The oral board will be testing your understanding and capacity, not your memory.

5) Get a good night's sleep and watch your general health and mental attitude

You will want a clear head at the interview. Take care of a cold or any other minor ailment, and of course, no hangovers.

What should be done on the day of the interview?

Now comes the day of the interview itself. Give yourself plenty of time to get there. Plan to arrive somewhat ahead of the scheduled time, particularly if your appointment is in the fore part of the day. If a previous candidate fails to appear, the board might be ready for you a bit early. By early afternoon an oral board is almost invariably behind schedule if there are many candidates, and you may have to wait. Take along a book or magazine to read, or your application to review, but leave any extraneous material in the waiting room when you go in for your interview. In any event, relax and compose yourself.

The matter of dress is important. The board is forming impressions about you – from your experience, your manners, your attitude, and your appearance. Give your personal appearance careful attention. Dress your best, but not your flashiest. Choose conservative, appropriate clothing, and be sure it is immaculate. This is a business interview, and your appearance should indicate that you regard it as such. Besides, being well groomed and properly dressed will help boost your confidence.

Sooner or later, someone will call your name and escort you into the interview room. *This is it.* From here on you are on your own. It is too late for any more preparation. But remember, you asked for this opportunity to prove your fitness, and you are here because your request was granted.

What happens when you go in?

The usual sequence of events will be as follows: The clerk (who is often the board stenographer) will introduce you to the chairman of the oral board, who will introduce you to the other members of the board. Acknowledge the introductions before you sit down. Do not be surprised if you find a microphone facing you or a stenotypist sitting by. Oral interviews are usually recorded in the event of an appeal or other review.

Usually the chairman of the board will open the interview by reviewing the highlights of your education and work experience from your application – primarily for the benefit of the other members of the board, as well as to get the material into the record. Do not interrupt or comment unless there is an error or significant misinterpretation; if that is the case, do not hesitate. But do not quibble about insignificant matters. Also, he will usually ask you some question about your education, experience or your present job – partly to get you to start talking and to establish the interviewing "rapport." He may start the actual questioning, or turn it over to one of the other members. Frequently, each member undertakes the questioning on a particular area, one in which he is perhaps most competent, so you can expect each member to participate in the examination. Because time is limited, you may also expect some rather abrupt switches in the direction the questioning takes, so do not be upset by it. Normally, a board member will not pursue a single line of questioning unless he discovers a particular strength or weakness.

After each member has participated, the chairman will usually ask whether any member has any further questions, then will ask you if you have anything you wish to add. Unless you are expecting this question, it may floor you. Worse, it may start you off on an extended, extemporaneous speech. The board is not usually seeking more information. The question is principally to offer you a last opportunity to present further qualifications or to indicate that you have nothing to add. So, if you feel that a significant qualification or characteristic has been overlooked, it is proper to point it out in a sentence or so. Do not compliment the board on the thoroughness of their examination – they have been sketchy, and you know it. If you wish, merely say, "No thank you, I have nothing further to add." This is a point where you can "talk yourself out" of a good impression or fail to present an important bit of information. Remember, *you close the interview yourself.*

The chairman will then say, "That is all, Mr. _____, thank you." Do not be startled; the interview is over, and quicker than you think. Thank him, gather your belongings and take your leave. Save your sigh of relief for the other side of the door.

How to put your best foot forward
Throughout this entire process, you may feel that the board individually and collectively is trying to pierce your defenses, seek out your hidden weaknesses and embarrass and confuse you. Actually, this is not true. They are obliged to make an appraisal of your qualifications for the job you are seeking, and they want to see you in your best light. Remember, they must interview all candidates and a non-cooperative candidate may become a failure in spite of their best efforts to bring out his qualifications. Here are 15 suggestions that will help you:

1) Be natural – Keep your attitude confident, not cocky
If you are not confident that you can do the job, do not expect the board to be. Do not apologize for your weaknesses, try to bring out your strong points. The board is interested in a positive, not negative, presentation. Cockiness will antagonize any board member and make him wonder if you are covering up a weakness by a false show of strength.

2) Get comfortable, but don't lounge or sprawl
Sit erectly but not stiffly. A careless posture may lead the board to conclude that you are careless in other things, or at least that you are not impressed by the importance of the occasion. Either conclusion is natural, even if incorrect. Do not fuss with your clothing, a pencil or an ashtray. Your hands may occasionally be useful to emphasize a point; do not let them become a point of distraction.

3) Do not wisecrack or make small talk
This is a serious situation, and your attitude should show that you consider it as such. Further, the time of the board is limited – they do not want to waste it, and neither should you.

4) Do not exaggerate your experience or abilities
In the first place, from information in the application or other interviews and sources, the board may know more about you than you think. Secondly, you probably will not get away with it. An experienced board is rather adept at spotting such a situation, so do not take the chance.

5) If you know a board member, do not make a point of it, yet do not hide it

Certainly you are not fooling him, and probably not the other members of the board. Do not try to take advantage of your acquaintanceship – it will probably do you little good.

6) Do not dominate the interview

Let the board do that. They will give you the clues – do not assume that you have to do all the talking. Realize that the board has a number of questions to ask you, and do not try to take up all the interview time by showing off your extensive knowledge of the answer to the first one.

7) Be attentive

You only have 20 minutes or so, and you should keep your attention at its sharpest throughout. When a member is addressing a problem or question to you, give him your undivided attention. Address your reply principally to him, but do not exclude the other board members.

8) Do not interrupt

A board member may be stating a problem for you to analyze. He will ask you a question when the time comes. Let him state the problem, and wait for the question.

9) Make sure you understand the question

Do not try to answer until you are sure what the question is. If it is not clear, restate it in your own words or ask the board member to clarify it for you. However, do not haggle about minor elements.

10) Reply promptly but not hastily

A common entry on oral board rating sheets is "candidate responded readily," or "candidate hesitated in replies." Respond as promptly and quickly as you can, but do not jump to a hasty, ill-considered answer.

11) Do not be peremptory in your answers

A brief answer is proper – but do not fire your answer back. That is a losing game from your point of view. The board member can probably ask questions much faster than you can answer them.

12) Do not try to create the answer you think the board member wants

He is interested in what kind of mind you have and how it works – not in playing games. Furthermore, he can usually spot this practice and will actually grade you down on it.

13) Do not switch sides in your reply merely to agree with a board member

Frequently, a member will take a contrary position merely to draw you out and to see if you are willing and able to defend your point of view. Do not start a debate, yet do not surrender a good position. If a position is worth taking, it is worth defending.

14) Do not be afraid to admit an error in judgment if you are shown to be wrong
The board knows that you are forced to reply without any opportunity for careful consideration. Your answer may be demonstrably wrong. If so, admit it and get on with the interview.

15) Do not dwell at length on your present job
The opening question may relate to your present assignment. Answer the question but do not go into an extended discussion. You are being examined for a *new* job, not your present one. As a matter of fact, try to phrase ALL your answers in terms of the job for which you are being examined.

Basis of Rating
Probably you will forget most of these "do's" and "don'ts" when you walk into the oral interview room. Even remembering them all will not ensure you a passing grade. Perhaps you did not have the qualifications in the first place. But remembering them will help you to put your best foot forward, without treading on the toes of the board members.
Rumor and popular opinion to the contrary notwithstanding, an oral board wants you to make the best appearance possible. They know you are under pressure – but they also want to see how you respond to it as a guide to what your reaction would be under the pressures of the job you seek. They will be influenced by the degree of poise you display, the personal traits you show and the manner in which you respond.

ABOUT THIS BOOK

This book contains tests divided into Examination Sections. Go through each test, answering every question in the margin. At the end of each test look at the answer key and check your answers. On the ones you got wrong, look at the right answer choice and learn. Do not fill in the answers first. Do not memorize the questions and answers, but understand the answer and principles involved. On your test, the questions will likely be different from the samples. Questions are changed and new ones added. If you understand these past questions you should have success with any changes that arise. Tests may consist of several types of questions. We have additional books on each subject should more study be advisable or necessary for you. Finally, the more you study, the better prepared you will be. This book is intended to be the last thing you study before you walk into the examination room. Prior study of relevant texts is also recommended. NLC publishes some of these in our Fundamental Series. Knowledge and good sense are important factors in passing your exam. Good luck also helps. So now study this Passbook, absorb the material contained within and take that knowledge into the examination. Then do your best to pass that exam.

EXAMINATION SECTION

EXAMINATION SECTION

TEST 1

DIRECTIONS: Each question or incomplete statement is followed by several suggested answers or completions. Select the one that BEST answers the question or completes the statement. *PRINT THE LETTER OF THE CORRECT ANSWER IN THE SPACE AT THE RIGHT.*

1. In programming, declaring a variable name involves what else other than naming?
   A. Type
   B. Length
   C. Size
   D. Style

   1._____

2. Name of a student is an example of
   A. operation
   B. method
   C. attribute
   D. none of the above

   2._____

3. Basic strength of a computer is
   A. speed
   B. memory
   C. accuracy
   D. reliability

   3._____

4. *Only girls can become members of the committee. Many of the members of the committee are officers. Some of the officers have been invited for dinner.*
   Based on the above statements, which is the CORRECT conclusion?
   A. All members of the committee have been invited for the dinner.
   B. Some officers are not girls.
   C. All girls are the members of the committee.
   D. None of the above

   4._____

5. Of the following statements, which of them cannot both be true and both be false?
   I. All babies cry
   II. Some babies cry
   III. No babies cry
   IV. Some babies do not cry

   The CORRECT answer is:
   A. I and II
   B. I and III
   C. III and IV
   D. I and IV

   5._____

6. 3, 7, 15, 31, 63, ? What number should come next?
   A. 83
   B. 127
   C. 122
   D. 76

   6._____

7. If 30% of a number is 12.6, find the number?
   A. 45
   B. 42
   C. 54
   D. 60

   7._____

8. 10, 25, 45, 54, 60, 75, 80. The odd one out is
   A. 10
   B. 45
   C. 54
   D. 60

   8._____

9. Complement of an input is produced by which logical function?
   A. AND
   B. OR
   C. NOT
   D. XOR

   9._____

10. *If marks are greater than 70 and less than 85, then the grade is B.*   10.____
   This statement is an example of which programming control structure?
   A. Decision   B. Loop
   C. Sequence   D. None of the above

11. In programming, which operator is called the assignment operator?   11.____
   A. +   B. =   C. _   D. %

12. In programming, which operator is called the modulus operator?   12.____
   A. +   B. =   C. %   D. /

13. What is the correct order of running a computer program?   13.____
   A. Linking, loading, execution, translation
   B. Loading, translation, execution, linking
   C. Execution, translation, linking, loading
   D. Translation, loading, linking, execution

14. In the case of structure of programming, which of the following terms means   14.____
   "if none of the other statements are true"?
   A. Else   B. Default   C. While   D. If

15. True statements: 15.____
   i. All benches are chairs.
   ii. Some chairs are desks.
   iii. All desks are pillars.
   Conclusions:
   I. Some pillars are benches.   II. Some pillars are chairs.
   III. Some desks are benches.   IV. No pillar is a bench.

   The CORRECT answer is:
   A. None of the above   B. Either I or IV, and III
   C. Either I or IV   D. Either I or IV, and II
   E. All of the above

16. True statements: 16.____
   i. Some snakes are reptiles.
   ii. All reptiles are poisonous.
   iii. Some poisonous reptiles are not snakes.
   Conclusions:
   I. Some poisonous reptiles are snakes.   II. All snakes are poisonous.
   III. All reptiles are snakes.   IV. No poisonous reptile is a snake.

   The CORRECT answer is:
   A. None of the above   B. Either I or IV, and III
   C. Either I or IV, and II   D. All of the above

17. Anna runs faster than Peter.
    Jane runs faster than Anna.
    Peter runs faster than Jane.
    If the first two statements are true, the third statement would be
       A. true   B. false   C. unknown   D. both

17._____

18. The sum of the digits of a two-digit number is 10. If the new number formed
    by reversing the digits is greater than the original number by 36, then what will
    be the original number?
       A. 37   B. 39   C. 57   D. 28

18._____

19. If an inverter is added to the output of an AND gate, what logic function is
    produced?
       A. AND   B. NAND   C. XOR   D. OR

19._____

20. Decimal 7 is represented by which gray code?
       A. 0111   B. 1011   C. 0100   D. 0101

20._____

21. According to propositional logic, if p = "A car costs less than $20,000", q =
    "David will buy a car."
    p → ~q refers to which of the following?
       A. If David will buy a car, the car costs less than $20,000.
       B. David will not buy a car if the car costs less than $20,000.
       C. David will buy a car if the car costs less than $20,000.
       D. None of the above

21._____

22. Which Boolean algebra rule is wrong?
       A. 0 + A = A   B. 0 + A = 1   C. A + A = A
       D. x • 1 = 1   E. All of the above

22._____

23. The 2's complement of 001011 is
       A. 110101   B. 010101   C. 110100   D. 010100

23._____

24. 7, 10, 8, 11, 9, 12. What number should come next?
       A. 12   B. 13   C. 8   D. 10

24._____

25. 2, 1, (1/2), (1/4). What number should come next?
       A. (1/16)   B. (1/8)   C. (2/8)   D. 1

25._____

KEY (CORRECT ANSWERS)

1.	A		11.	B
2.	C		12.	C
3.	B		13.	D
4.	D		14.	B
5.	B		15.	C
6.	B		16.	C
7.	B		17.	B
8.	C		18.	A
9.	C		19.	B
10.	A		20.	C

21.	B
22.	B
23.	A
24.	D
25.	B

TEST 2

DIRECTIONS: Each question or incomplete statement is followed by several suggested answers or completions. Select the one that BEST answers the question or completes the statement. *PRINT THE LETTER OF THE CORRECT ANSWER IN THE SPACE AT THE RIGHT.*

1. 8, 27, 64, 100, 125, 216, 343. The odd one out is   1.____
   A. 343   B. 8   C. 27   D. 100

2. In programming, what is the operator precedence?   2.____
   A. Arithmetic, comparison, logical
   B. Comparison, arithmetic, logical
   C. Arithmetic, logical, comparison
   D. Logical, arithmetic, comparison

3. Which of the following is NOT a type of programming error?   3.____
   A. Logical   B. Syntax   C. Superficial   D. Runtime

4. Statements: 4.____
   i. No man is good.   ii. Jack is a man.
   Conclusions:
   I. Jack is not good   II. All men are not Jack.

   The CORRECT answer is:
   A. I   B. II
   C. Either I or II   D. Neither I nor II
   E. Both I and II

5. Statements: 5.____
   i. All students are boys.   ii. No boy is dull.
   Conclusions:
   I. There are no girls in the class.   II. No student is dull.

   The CORRECT answer is:
   A. I   B. II
   C. Either I or II   D. Neither I nor II
   E. Both I and II

6. What is the sum of two consecutive even numbers, the difference of whose squares is 84?   6.____
   A. 32   B. 36   C. 40   D. 42

7. Choose the odd one out:

(1)   (2)   (3)   (4)

   A. 1   B. 2   C. 3   D. 4

7.____

8. In the Netherlands, almost 200 cyclists die each year on the road.
Head injury is the main cause of death among cyclists.
Which of the following statements is true based on the above information?
   A. In the Netherlands, if wearing a helmet was widespread among cyclists, the number of deaths in cyclists could be reduced.
   B. Too many cyclists die each year on the road in the Netherlands.
   C. Most deaths in the Netherlands occur due to cycling.
   D. None of the above

8.____

9. According to propositional logic, what is the order of precedence of operators?
   A. ^, v, ↔, →
   B. ~, ^, v, →, ↔
   C. ~, v, ^, ↔, →
   D. →, ~, ^, v, ↔

9.____

10. The binary equivalent of the number 50 is
   A. 01101   B. 11010   C. 11100   D. 110010

10.____

11. Number 200 can be represented by how many bits?
   A. 1   B. 5   C. 8   D. 10

11.____

12. Which of the following is NOT true?
   A. $0 \times 0 = 0$ B. $1 \times 0 = 0$ C. $0 \times 1 = 1$ D. $1 \times 1 = 1$

12.____

13. Get two numbers
If first number is bigger than second then
Print first number
Else
Print second number
The above pseudo-code is an example of which control structure?
   A. Loop   B. Sequence
   C. Decision   D. None of the above

13.____

14. A group of variables is called
   A. data structure   B. control structure
   C. data object   D. linked list

14.____

15. The first character of the string variable St is represented by
   A. St[1]   B. St[0]
   C. St   D. none of the above

15.____

16. Statements:
    i. No girl is poor
    Conclusions:
    I. No poor girl is rich

    B. All girls are rich

    II. No rich girl is poor

    The CORRECT answer is:
    A. I
    C. Either I or II
    E. Both I and II

    B. II
    D. Neither I nor II

16._____

17. Statements:
    i. All fishes are orange in color
    Conclusions:
    I. All heavy fishes are orange in color
    II. All light fishes are not orange in color

    ii. Some fishes are heavy

    The CORRECT answer is:
    A. I
    C. Either I or II
    E. Both I and II

    B. II
    D. Neither I nor II

17._____

18. 3, 7, 6, 5, 9, 3, 12, 1, 15. What number should come next?
    A. 18   B. 13   C. 1   D. -1

18._____

19. 5184, 1728, 576, 192. What number should come next?
    A. 64   B. 32   C. 120   D. 44

19._____

20. $(p \Leftrightarrow r) \Rightarrow (q \Leftrightarrow r)$ is equivalent to
    A. $[(\sim p \lor r) \land (p \lor \sim r)] \lor \sim [(\sim q \lor r) \land (q \lor \sim r)]$
    B. $\sim[(\sim p \lor r) \land (p \lor \sim r)] \lor [(\sim q \lor r) \land (q \lor \sim r)]$
    C. $[(\sim p \lor r) \land (p \lor \sim r)] \land [(\sim q \lor r) \land (q \lor \sim r)]$
    D. $[(\sim p \lor r) \land (p \lor \sim r)] \lor [(\sim q \lor r) \land (q \lor \sim r)]$

20._____

21. Which of the following propositions is a tautology?
    A. $(p \lor q) \to q$ B. $p \lor (q \to p)$ C. $p \lor (p \to q)$ D. b & c

21._____

22. According to propositional logic, if p = "Mary gets an A in computer science",
    q = "Mary got 90% marks in computer science."
    $p \leftrightarrow q$ refers to which of the following?
    A. Mary gets an A in computer science if and only if her percentage in
        computer science is 90%.
    B. Mary might get an A in computer science if her percentage in computer
        science is 90%
    C. Mary get an A in computer science if her percentage in computer science
        is 90%.
    D. None of the above

22._____

7

23. What does the following flowchart depict?

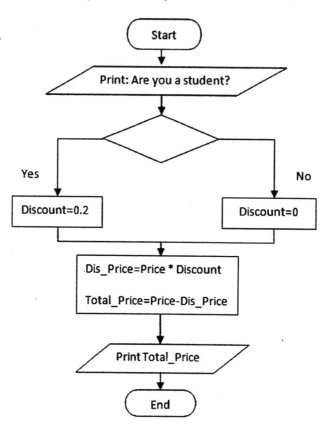

A. All users get a discount.
B. If user is a student, only then does he get a discount.
C. If user is a student, he does not get a discount, while other users get a discount.
D. None of the above

24. 13, 35, 57, 79, 911. What number should come next?

    A. 1113   B. 1114   C. 1100   D. 1111

25. Choose the missing shape.

25.____

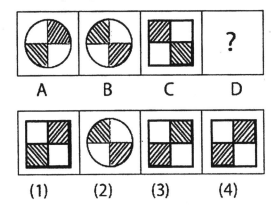

A   B   C   D

(1)   (2)   (3)   (4)

A. 1   B. 2   C. 3   D. 4

KEY (CORRECT ANSWERS)

1.	D	11.	C
2.	A	12.	C
3.	C	13.	C
4.	A	14.	A
5.	E	15.	B
6.	D	16.	E
7.	A	17.	A
8.	A	18.	D
9.	B	19.	A
10.	D	20.	B

21.	D
22.	A
23.	B
24.	C
25.	C

9

TEST 3

DIRECTIONS: Each question or incomplete statement is followed by several suggested answers or completions. Select the one that BEST answers the question or completes the statement. *PRINT THE LETTER OF THE CORRECT ANSWER IN THE SPACE AT THE RIGHT.*

1. The following flowchart represents which control structure?   1.____

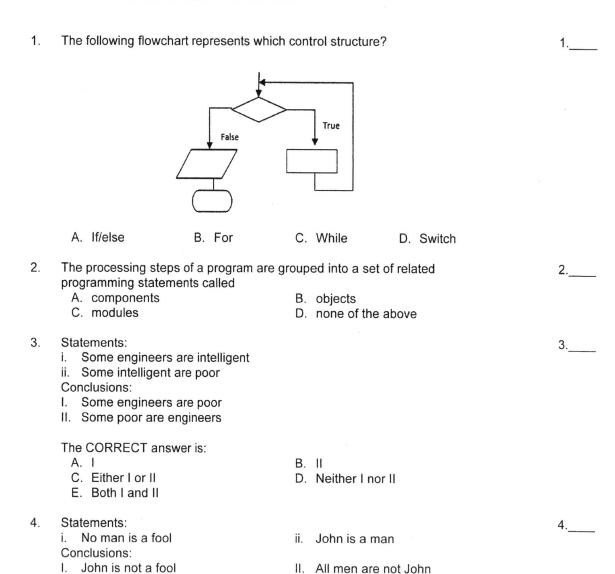

    A. If/else   B. For   C. While   D. Switch

2. The processing steps of a program are grouped into a set of related   2.____
programming statements called
    A. components   B. objects
    C. modules   D. none of the above

3. Statements: 3.____
    i. Some engineers are intelligent
    ii. Some intelligent are poor
  Conclusions:
    I. Some engineers are poor
    II. Some poor are engineers

  The CORRECT answer is:
    A. I   B. II
    C. Either I or II   D. Neither I nor II
    E. Both I and II

4. Statements: 4.____
    i. No man is a fool   ii. John is a man
  Conclusions:
    I. John is not a fool   II. All men are not John

  The CORRECT answer is:
    A. I   B. II
    C. Either I or II   D. Neither I nor II
    E. Both I and II

5. John weighs less than Fred.
    John weighs more than Boomer.
    Of the three dogs, Boomer weighs the least.

    If the first two statements are true, the third statement is
       A. true   B. false   C. uncertain   D. both

    5.____

6. A file contains 10 sheets and none of these sheets is blue. Which of the
    following statements can be deduced?
       A. None of the 10 sheets contained in the file are blue.
       B. The file contains a blue sheet.
       C. The file contains at least one yellow sheet.
       D. None of the above

    6.____

7. Choose the odd one out:

        (1)   (2)   (3)   (4)

       A. 1   B. 2   C. 3   D. 4

    7.____

8. Which of the following structures requires the statements to be repeated
    until a condition is met?
       A. Sequence   B. If....Else
       C. For   D. None of the above

    8.____

9. While n is greater than 0
    Increment count
    end
    The above pseudo-code represents which programming structure?
       A. Sequence   B. Loop
       C. Structure   D. None of the above

    9.____

10. Which of the following converts a source code into machine code and
    turns it into an exe file?
       A. Linker   B. Compiler
       C. Interpreter   D. None of the above

    10.____

11. Which of the following is used to hide data and its functionality?
       A. Structure   B. Loop
       C. Object   D. Selection statement

    11.____

12. Statements:
    i.   All apples are golden in color
    ii. No golden colored things are cheap
    Conclusions:
    I.   All apples are cheap
    II. Golden colored apples are not cheap

    The CORRECT answer is:
    A. I   B. II
    C. Either I or II   D. Neither I nor II
    E. Both I and II

12._____

13. Statements:
    i.   All cups are glasses
    ii.   All glasses are bowls
    iii. No bowl is a plate
    Conclusions:
    I.   No cup is a plate   II. No glass is a plate
    III. Some plates are bowls   IV. Some cups are not glasses

    The CORRECT answer is:
    A. None of the above   B. Either I or IV, and III
    C. Either I or IV   D. Either I or IV, and II
    E. All of the above

13._____

14. 331, 482, 551, 263, 383, 362, 284. The odd one out is
    A. 331   B. 383   C. 284   D. 551

14._____

15. 3, 5, 7, 12, 17, 19. The odd one out is
    A. 7   B. 17   C. 12   D. 19

15._____

16. Ratio of 12 minutes to 1 hour is:
    A. 2:3   B. 1:5   C. 1:6   D. 1:8

16._____

17. 10 cats caught 10 rats in 10 seconds. How many cats are required to catch
    100 rats in 100 seconds?
    A. 100   B. 50   C. 200   D. 10

17._____

18. Four engineers and six technicians can complete a project in 8 days,
    while three engineers and seven technicians can complete it in 10 days. In
    how many days will ten technicians complete it?
    A. 40   B. 36   C. 50   D. 45

18._____

19. According to propositional logic, if p = "Jane is smart", "q = "Jane is honest",
    then p ∨ (~p ∧ q) refers to which of the following?
    A. Either Jane is smart or honest.
    B. Jane is smart and honest.
    C. Either Jane is smart, or she is not smart but honest.
    D. None of the above

19._____

20. In binary number system, the number 102 is equal to   20.____
    A. 1100110   B. 1001100   C. 1110110   D. 1100101

21. In base 8, number 362 is represented as   21.____
    A. 550   B. 552   C. 545   D. 566

22. 396, 462, 572, 427, 671, 264. The odd one out is   22.____
    A. 427   B. 572   C. 671   D. 264

23. A is two years older than B who is twice as old as C. If the total of the   23.____
ages of A, B and C is 27, then how old is B?
    A. 10   B. 11   C. 12   D. 13

24. What is 50% of 40% of Rs. 3,450?   24.____
    A. 580   B. 670   C. 690   D. 570

25. What is the minimum number of colors required to fill the spaces in the   25.____
following diagram without the adjacent sides having the same color?

A. 3   B. 4
C. 6   D. Not possible to determine

KEY (CORRECT ANSWERS)

1.	A		11.	A
2.	C		12.	B
3.	E		13.	A
4.	A		14.	D
5.	A		15.	C
6.	A		16.	B
7.	D		17.	D
8.	C		18.	A
9.	B		19.	C
10.	B		20.	A

21.	B
22.	A
23.	A
24.	C
25.	A

TEST 4

DIRECTIONS: Each question or incomplete statement is followed by several suggested answers or completions. Select the one that BEST answers the question or completes the statement. *PRINT THE LETTER OF THE CORRECT ANSWER IN THE SPACE AT THE RIGHT.*

1. Computer signals that include both measuring and counting are called
   A. analog
   B. digital
   C. hybrid
   D. none of the above

   1.____

2. The result of ANDing 5 and 4 is
   A. 30
   B. 9
   C. 20
   D. none of the above

   2.____

3. If one wants to trace an organization's purchase orders from creation to final disposition, he should use which of the following?
   A. Data flow diagram
   B. Internal control flow chart
   C. System flow chart
   D. Program flow chart

   3.____

4. Statements:
   i. Some tables are sofas
   ii. All furniture are tables
   Conclusions:
   I. Some furniture are sofas
   II. Some sofas are furniture

   The two statements given should be assumed to be true. Select the conclusion.
   A. I
   B. II
   C. Either I or II
   D. Neither I nor II
   E. Both I and II

   4.____

5. Statements:
   i. Many actors are singers.
   ii. All singers are dancers.
   Conclusions:
   I. Some actors are dancers.
   II. No singer is an actor.

   The CORRECT answer is:
   A. I
   B. II
   C. Either I or II
   D. Neither I nor II
   E. Both I and II

   5.____

6. Anna will not pass both the verbal reasoning test and quantitative reasoning test. This statement refers to which of the following?
   A. Anna will not pass the verbal reasoning test.
   B. Anna will neither pass quantitative reasoning test nor verbal reasoning test.
   C. Anna will pass either the verbal reasoning test or the numerical reasoning test.
   D. If Anna passes the verbal reasoning test, she will not pass the numerical reasoning test.

   6.____

7. Which symbol is used at the beginning of the flowchart?

A. ○   B. ⬭   C. ◇   D. ▭

7.____

8. A list of instructions in a proper order to solve a problem is called
   A. sequence
   C. flowchart
   B. algorithm
   D. none of the above

8.____

9. Statements:
   i.   Some pearls are stones
   ii. Some stones are diamonds
   iii. No diamond is a gem
   Conclusions:
   I.   Some gems are pearls
   III. No gem is a diamond
   II. Some gems are diamonds
   IV. No gem is a pearl

   The CORRECT answer is:
   A. None of the above
   C. Either I or IV
   E. All of the above
   B. Either I or IV, and III
   D. Either I or IV, and II

9.____

10. 53, 53, 40, 40, 27, 27. What number should come next?
    A. 14   B. 12   C. 13   D. 10

10.____

11. 1, 3, 1, 9, 1, 81, 1. What number should come next?
    A. 4   B. 1   C. 343   D. 6561

11.____

12. A father is 30 years older than his son. He will be three times as old as
    his son after 5 years. What is the father's present age?
    A. 30   B. 35   C. 40   D. 45

12.____

13. Ahmed is older than Ali
    Maria is older than Ahmed.
    Ali is older than Maria.
    If the first two statements are true, the third statement is
    A. true   B. false   C. unknown   D. both

13.____

14. All flowers are fruit.
    Some flowers are leaves.
    All leaves are fruit.
    If the first two statements are true, the third statement is
    A. true   B. false   C. unknown   D. both

14.____

15. The Spring Mall has more stores than the Four Seasons Mall.
    The Four Corners Mall has fewer stores than the Four Seasons Mall.
    The Spring Mall has more stores than the Four Corners Mall.
    If the first two statements are true, the third statement is
    A. true   B. false   C. unknown   D. both

15.____

16. Choose the odd one out:

(1)   (2)   (3)   (4)

    A. 1   B. 2   C. 3   D. 4

16.____

17. Fact 1: All cats like to jump.
Fact 2: Some cats like to run.
Fact 3: Some cats look like dogs.
If the first three statements are true, which of the following statements must also be true?
I.   All cats who like to jump look like dogs.
II. Cats who like to run also like to jump.
III. Cats who like to jump do not look like dogs.

The CORRECT answer is:
    A. I only   B. II only
    C. II and III only   D. None of the above

17.____

18. Fact 1: All chickens are birds.
Fact 2: Some chickens are hens.
Fact 3: Female birds lay eggs.
If the first three statements are true, which of the following statements must also be true?
I.   All birds lay eggs.
II. Some hens are birds.
III. Some chickens are not hens.

The CORRECT answer is:
    A. I only   B. II only
    C. II and III only   D. None of the above

18.____

19. Fact 1: Jake has four watches.
Fact 2: Two of the watches are black.
Fact 3: One of the watches is a Rolex.
If the first three statements are true, which of the following statements must also be true?
I.   Jake has a Rolex.
II. Jake has three watches.
III. Jake's favorite color is black.

The CORRECT answer is:
    A. I only   B. II only
    C. II and III only   D. None of the above

19.____

20. Which symbol of a flowchart is used to test a condition?

    A. ◯   B. ⟋⟋   C. ◇   D. ⬭

21. Which symbol of a flowchart is used for input and output?

    A. ◯   B. ⟋⟋   C. ◇   D. ▭

22. Which of the following is NOT one of the categories of flowcharting symbols?
    A. Input/output symbols   B. Processing symbols
    C. Storage symbols   D. Flow symbols

23. Choose the missing shape.

    A. 1   B. 2   C. 3   D. 4

24. Choose the missing shape.

    A. 1   B. 2   C. 3   D. 4

25. How many minimum numbers of colors will be required to fill a cube without adjacent sides having the same color?   25.____
    A. 3   · B. 4   C. 6   D. 8

KEY (CORRECT ANSWERS)

1.	C		11.	D
2.	C		12.	C
3.	B		13.	B
4.	E		14.	C
5.	A		15.	A
6.	B		16.	A
7.	B		17.	B
8.	B		18.	B
9.	B		19.	A
10.	A		20.	C

21.	B
22.	C
23.	B
24.	A
25.	A

EXAMINATION SECTION
TEST 1

DIRECTIONS: Each question or incomplete statement is followed by several suggested answers or completions. Select the one that BEST answers the question or completes the statement. *PRINT THE LETTER OF THE CORRECT ANSWER IN THE SPACE AT THE RIGHT.*

Questions 1-10.

DIRECTIONS: Answer question 1 through 10 on the basis of the following set of instructions, including the sample program.

1. A plus sign (+) means that you add the two values on either side of the plus sign.

2. A minus sign (-) means that you subtract the value at the right of the minus sign from the value at the left of the minus sign.

3. An equal sign (=) means that the computed value of everything to the left of the equal sign is the same in value as the computed value of everything to the right of the equal sign.

4. All statements (for example, see Sample Program) are executed in Statement Number order unless there is an Instruction directing you to go to another Statement Number.

5. GO TO means that you proceed to the program statement indicatec in that Instruction. The word IF in such a statement means that you proceed to the program statement indicated only if the conditions specified are met.

6. The symbol > means *is greater than.*

7. The symbol < means *is less than.*

8. <u>Sample Program</u>

<u>Statement No</u>.	<u>Instruction,</u>
10	C = B + A
20	D = C + F
30	IF D > 20 THEN GO TO 50
40	D = B - A
50	END

<u>Explanation</u>

Assume that you are given the values

A = 10,
B = 5, and
F = 8.

It can be seen that when the Instruction for Statement No. 10 has been carried out, C = 15. After the Instruction for Statement No. 10 is completed, D = 23. On the basis of Instruction 30, you proceed to Instruction 50 because D is greater than 20. Instruction 40 is not executed because Instruction 30 directed you to proceed to Instruction 50, which terminates the program.

Questions 1-5.

DIRECTIONS: Answer questions 1 through 5 on the basis of the following program:

Statement No.	Instruction
10	C = B - A
20	D = C + B
30	GO TO 60
40	F = B + C
50	GO TO 80
60	F = D + A
70	IF F > 10 THEN GO TO 40, OTHERWISE GO TO 80
80	END

1.   If A = 1 and B = 1, what is the value of F?

    A.   0   B.   1   C.   2   D.   3

1.____

2.   If A = 10 and B = 15, what is the value of F?

    A.   10   B.   20   C.   30   D.   40

2.____

3.   If A = 0 and B = 0, what is the value of F?

    A.   -1   B.   0   C.   1   D.   2

3.____

4.   If A = -2 and B = -2, what is the value of F?

    A.   -5   B.   -4   C.   -3   D.   0

4.____

5.   If A = -5 and B = 6, what is the value of F?

    A.   0   B.   17   C.   19   D.   20

5.____

Questions 6-10.

DIRECTIONS: Answer questions 6 through 10 on the basis of the following program:

Statement No.	Instruction
10	C = A - B
20	D = B + C
30	IF D > 0 THEN GO TO 90
40	IF D < 0 THEN GO TO 70
50	E = D - C
60	GO TO 100
70	E = C - D
80	GO TO 100
90	E = C + D
100	END

6.   If A = 2 and B = 4, what is the value of E?

    A.   5   B.   4   C.   1   D.   0

6.____

7.   If A = 4 and B = 2, what is the value of E?

    A.   2   B.   4   C.   6   D.   8

7.____

8.   If A = 3 and B = 3, what is the value of E?

    A.   -3   B.   -2   C.   0   D.   3

8.____

9.   If A = -1 and B = 1, what is the value of E?   9._____

 A. -2   B. -1   C. 0   D. 1

10.   If A = 0 and B = 0, what is the value of E?   10._____

 A. -1   B. 0   C. 2   D. 3

Questions 11 - 16.

DIRECTIONS: Answer questions 11 through 16 on the basis of the following rules for calculating Tax Withheld from Weekly Salary.

1.   Tax Withheld is computed by multiplying the Taxable Income by the appropriate Tax Rate indicated below.

 0% for Taxable Incomes from $ 1.01 to $ 50,000
 3% for Taxable Incomes from $50.01 to $ 70,00
 5% for Taxable Incomes from $70.01 to $100.00
 6% for Taxable Incomes   OVER $100.00

2.   Taxable Income is equal to Gross Salary less Exemptions.

3.   Exemptions are equal to $10 multiplied by the Number of Dependents

4.   Gross Salary is equal to Base Pay plus Overtime Pay.

5.   Base Pay is equal to Hourly Wage Rate multiplied by the number of Regular Hours worked.

6.   Overtime Pay is equal to 11/2 times the Hourly Wage Rate multiplied by the number of Overtime Hours worked.

7.   Regular Hours is equal to the total number of hours worked Monday through Saturday up to a maximum of 8 hours on any day.

8.   Overtime Hours is equal to any hours worked on Sunday plus any hours worked in excess of 8 hours on any day or in excess of 40 hours in any week.

11.   Which of the following represents a list of things which must be known in order to accurately calculate Gross Salary?   11._____

 A.   Number of Dependents and Hourly Wage Rate
 B.   Taxable Income and Base Pay
 C.   Hourly Wage Rate, Regular Hours, and Overtime Hours
 D.   Hourly Wage Rate, Total Hours, and Number of Dependents

12.   According to the rules, Taxable Income can be properly calculated only by knowing   12._____

 A.   Overtime Hours, Regular Hours, and Tax Rate
 B.   Gross Salary Tax Rate
 C.   Gross Salary and Number of Dependents
 D.   Tax Rate and Exemptions

13. To calculate the Tax Withheld, we must   13.____

    A. apply the appropriate Tax Rate to Gross Salary
    B. subtract the Exemptions from Taxable Income before applying the appropriate Tax Rate
    C. subtract Exemptions from Taxable Income after applying the appropriate Tax Rate
    D. subtract Exemptions from Gross Salary before applying the appropriate Tax Rate

14. On the basis of the above rules, the Tax Rate that will be applied to a person with a Gross Salary of $100 and 7 Dependents is   14.____

    A. 0%   B. 3%   C. 5%   D. 6%

15. If a person worked 8 hours Monday through Friday, and 6 hours on Saturday, one way of calculating his Gross Salary is multiply his Hourly Wage Rate by   15.____

    A. 46
    B. 49
    C. 1 1/2 and then multiply the result by 40
    D. 1 1/2 and then multiply the result by 46

16. If a person worked 8 hours Wednesday and Thursday, 10 hours Friday and Saturday, and no hours on any other day that week, his Overtime Hours would be   16.____

    A. 0   B. 4   C. 10   D. 20

Questions 17 - 20.

DIRECTIONS: Answer question 17 through 20 on the basis of the following account of a department store's billing procedure.

The amount billed the customer, called the NEW BALANCE, is calculated by the following method:

NEW BALANCE = LAST MONTH'S BALANCE
less   all RETURNS and CREDITS
less   PAYMENTS
plus   NEW PURCHASES
plus   FINANCE CHARGE

The FINANCE CHARGE is equal to the FINANCE RATE multiplied by the AMOUNT SUBJECT TO FINANCE CHARGES.
The FINANCE RATE is regulated by law. In this example the rate used is 1 1/2% per month on the first $500 and 1% per month on only that amount which is in excess of $500. The AMOUNT SUBJECT TO FINANCE CHARGES is defined as:

LAST MONTH'S BALANCE less RETURNS and CREDITS plus NEW PURCHASES

17. If the AMOUNT SUBJECT TO FINANCE CHARGE ia $637, the correct method for calculating FINANCE CHARGE is   17.____

    A. 1% of $637
    B. 1 1/2% of $637
    C. 1 1/2% of $500 plus 1% of $637
    D. 1 1/2% of $500 plus 1% of $137

18. To properly calculate FINANCE CHARGE, before multiplying by FINANCE RATE it is necessary to   18._____

    A. subtract PAYMENTS, CREDITS and RETURNS from LAST MONTH'S BALANCE
    B. add PURCHASES to and subtract PAYMENTS, CREDITS and RETURNS from LAST MONTH'S BALANCE
    C. add PURCHASES to LAST MONTH'S BALANCE
    D. add PURCHASES to and subtract CREDITS and RETURNS from LAST MONTH'S BALANCE

19. If the department store wanted to change its method of determining the AMOUNT SUBJECT TO FINANCE CHARGES so as to derive maximum income from the FINANCE CHARGE paid by their customers, which of the following methods for determining the AMOUNT SUBJECT TO FINANCE CHARGES would be used?   19._____

    A. AMOUNT SUBJECT TO FINANCE CHARGES - LAST MONTH'S BALANCE plus NEW PURCHASES
    B. AMOUNT SUBJECT TO FINANCE CHARGE = NEW BALANCE
    C. AMOUNT SUBJECT TO FINANCE CHARGE = LAST MONTH'S BALANCE
    D. AMOUNT SUBJECT TO FINANCE CHARGE = LAST MONTH'S BALANCE less PAYMENTS, RETURNS and CREDITS

20. If there were no new purchases during the period billed, the AMOUNT SUBJECT TO FINANCE CHARGES would be   20._____

    A. LAST MONTH'S BALANCE
    B. LAST MONTH'S BALANCE less PAYMENTS
    C. LAST MONTH'S BALANCE less PAYMENTS, CREDITS and RETURNS
    D. LAST MONTH'S BALANCE less CREDITS and RETURNS

Questions 21 - 27.

DIRECTIONS: Answer questions 21 through 27 on the basis of the following passage.

The first step in establishing a programming development schedule is to rate the programs to be developed or to be maintained on the basis of complexity, size, and input-output complexity. The most experienced programmer should rate the program complexity based on the system flow chart. The same person should do all of the rating so that all programs are rated in the same manner. If possible, the same person who rates the complexity should estimate the program size based on the number of pages of coding. This rating can easily be checked, after coding has been completed, against the number of pages of coding actually produced. If there is consistent error in the estimates for program size, all future estimates should be corrected for this error or the estimating method reviewed.

The input-output rating is a mechanical count of the number of input and output units or tapes which the program uses. The objective is to measure the number of distinct files which the program must control.
After the ratings have been completed, the man-days required for each of the tasks can be calculated. Good judgment, or, if available, a table of past experience, is used to translate the ratings into man-days, the units which the schedule is expressed. The calculations should keep the values for each task completely separate so that a later evaluation can be made by program, programmer, and function.

After the values have been calculated, it is simple matter to establish a development schedule. This can be a simple bar chart which assigns work to specific programmers, a complex computer program using the PERT technique of critical path scheduling, or other useful type of document.

21. The rating and estimating of the programs should be performed by   21.____

    A. the person who will do the programming
    B. a programmer trainee
    C. the most experienced programmer
    D. the operations supervisor

22. The measurement used, to express the programming schedule is the number of   22.____

    A. distinct files controlled by the programmer
    B. man-days
    C. pages of coding
    D. programmers

23. A mechanical count of the number of input and output units or tapes should be considered as a(n)   23.____

    A. input-output rating
    B. measure of the number of man-days required
    C. rating of complexity
    D. estimate of the number of pages of coding

24. Programming development scheduling methods are for   24.____

    A. new programs only
    B. programs to be developed and maintained
    C. large and complicated programs only
    D. maintenance programs only

25. If there is a consistent error in the estimates for program size, all estimates should be   25.____

    A. adjusted for future programs
    B. eliminated for all programs
    C. replaced by rating of complexity
    D. replaced by input-output rating

26. It is INTIMATED that   26.____

    A. the calculations should keep the valuations for each task completely separated
    B. it is a simple matter to establish a development schedule
    C. the man-days required for each of the tasks can be calculated
    D. a later evaluation will be made

27. Complexity of programs can be checked   27.____

    A. before coding has been completed
    B. after future estimates have been corrected for error
    C. as a first stop in establishing a complex computer program
    D. with reference to the number of pages of coding produced

Questions 28 - 33.

DIRECTIONS: Answer questions 28 through 33 on the basis of the following passage.

The purposes of program testing are to determine that the program has been coded correctly, that the coding matches the logical design, and that the logical design matches the basic requirements of the job as set down in the specifications. Program errors fall into the following categories: errors in logic, clerical errors, misidentification of the computer components' functions, misinterpretation of the requirements of the job, and system analysis errors.

The number of errors in a program will average one for each 125 instructions, assuming that the programmer has been reasonably careful in his coding system, The number of permutations and combinations of conditions in a program may reach into the billions before each possibility has been thoroughly checked out. It is therefore a practical impossibility to check out each and every possible combination of conditions -- the effort would take years, even in the simplest program. As a result, it is quite possible for errors to remain latent for a number of years, suddenly appearing when a particular combination is reached which had not previously occurred.

Latent program errors will remain in operating programs, and their occurrence should be minimized by complete and thorough testing. The fact that the program is operative and reaches end-of-job satisfactorily does not mean that all of the exception conditions, and their permutations and combinations have been tested. Quite the contrary, many programs reach end-of-job after very few tests, since the STRAIGHT-LINE part of the program is often simplest. However, the exceptions programmed to deal with a minimal percentage of the input account for a large percentage of the instructions. It is therefore quite possible to reach the end-of-job halt with only 10% of the program checked out.

28. One of the MAIN points of this passage is that   28._____

    A.   it is impossible to do a good job of programming
    B.   reaching end-of-job means only 10% of the program is checked out
    C.   standard testing procedures should require testing of every possible combination of conditions
    D.   elimination of all errors can never be assured, but the occurrecne of errors can be minimized by thorough testing

29. Latent program errors GENERALLY   29._____

    A.   evade detection for some time
    B.   are detected in the last test run
    C.   test the number of permutations and combinations in a program
    D.   allow the program to go to end-of-job

30. Which one of the following statements, pertaining to errors in a program is CORRECT?   30._____

    A.   If the program has run to a normal completion, then all program errors have been eliminated.
    B.   Program errors, if not caught in testing, will surely be detected in the first hundred runs of the program.
    C.   It is practically impossible to verify that the typical program is free of errors.
    D.   A program that is coded correctly is free of errors.

31. Among other things, program testing is designed to

A. assure that the documentation is correct
B. assure that the coding is correct
C. determine the program running time
D. measure programmer's performance

32. The difficulty in detecting errors in programs is due to

A. the extremely large number of conditions that exist in a program
B. poor analysis of work errors
C. very sophisticated and clever programming
D. reaching the end-of-job halt with only 10% of the program checked out

33. If the program being tested finally reaches the end-of-job halt it means that

A. one path through the program has been successfully tested
B. less than 10% of the program has been tested
C. the program has been coded correctly
D. the logical design is correct

Questions 34 - 40.

DIRECTIONS: Answer questions 34 through 40 on the basis of the following passage.

Systems analysis represents a major link in the chain of transe-lations from the problem to its machine solution. After the problem and its requirements for solution have been stated in clear terms, the systems analyst defines the broad outlines of the machine solution. He must know the overall capabilities of the equipment, and he must be familiar with the application. The ultimate output of the analysis is a detailed job specification containing all the tools necessary to produce a series of computer programs. The purpose of the specifications is to document and describe the system by defining the problem and the proposed solution, explain system outputs and functions, state system requirements for programmers and to avoid misunderstandings among involved departments. The specification serves as the link between the analysis of the problem and the next function, programming. Systems analysis relies on creativity rather than rote analysis to develop effective computer systems. But this creativity must be channeled and documented effectively if lasting value is to be obtained.

34. According to the above paragraph, the systems analyst must be familiar with

A. programming and the maching solution
B. the machine solution and the next function
C. the application and programming
D. the application and the equipment capabilities

35. According to the above paragraph, the time that systems analysis must be performed is

A. after the problem analysis
B. after programming
C. before problem definition
D. before problem analysis

36. According to the above paragraph, the MAIN task performed by the systems analyst is to   36.____

     A. write the program
     B. analyze the problem
     C. define the overall capacities of the equipment
     D. define the machine solution of the problem

37. According to the above paragraph, the document produced by the systems analyst as his   37.____
main output does NOT normally include

     A. an explanation of system outputs
     B. system requirements for programmers
     C. a statement of the problem
     D. performance standards

38. According to the above paragraph, the systems analysis function is   38.____

     A. relatively straightforward, requiring little creative effort
     B. extremely complex, making standard procedures impossible
     C. primarily a rote memory procedure
     D. a creative effort

39. According to the above paragraph, the specification   39.____

     A. is a major link in the sequence from problem to machine solution
     B. states the problem and its requirements for solution
     C. is chiefly concerned with the overall capabilities of the equipment
     D. represents the ultimate product of systems analysis

40. According to the above paragraph, the sequential function after the analysis of the pro-   40.____
gram is

     A. documentation   B. application
     C. definition   D. programming

KEY (CORRECT ANSWERS)

1.	C	11.	C	21.	C	31.	B
2.	B	12.	C	22.	B	32.	A
3.	B	13.	D	23.	A	33.	A
4.	B	14.	A	24.	B	34.	D
5.	B	15.	B	25.	A	35.	A
6.	D	16.	B	26.	D	36.	D
7.	C	17.	D	27.	D	37.	D
8.	D	18.	D	28.	D	38.	D
9.	B	19.	A	29.	A	39.	D
10.	B	20.	D	30.	C	40.	D

TEST 2

DIRECTIONS: Each question or incomplete statement is followed by several suggested answers or completions. Select the one that BEST answers the question or completes the statement. *PRINT THE LETTER OF THE CORRECT ANSWER IN THE SPACE AT THE RIGHT.*

1. A cube-shaped box has a side of S inches. The volume of the box is S^3 cubic inches. If each side of the box were increased by 3 inches, the volume would then be represented by   1._____

    A. $(S+3)^3$ B. S^3+3 C. $(3S+9)^3$ D. S^3+3^3

2. In an agency, 7/12 of the employees are engaged in clerical work, 1/3 of the employees are engaged in supervisory work, and 1/4 of the employees are NOT engaged in either clerical or supervisory work.
How many employees in this agency are engaged in BOTH clerical and supervisory work?   2._____

    A. 1/6   B. 1/12   C. 1/3   D. 1/4

3. A new computer installation has the memory capacity to run 15 jobs simultaneously, whereas the old computer installation has the memory capacity to run 5 jobs simultaneously.
If it took the old computer 2 hours and 36 minutes to run 250 jobs, how long will it take the new computer to run 625 jobs, assuming it takes the same amount of time for both computers to run each single job?   3._____

    A. 52 minutes   B. 1 hour 30 minutes
    C. 1 hour 50 minutes   D. 2 hours 10 minutes

4. In a right triangle, the area is equal to 1/2 the product of two legs. Assume you have the following five right triangles with legs as indicated: 4._____
    Triangle I,   legs 9 inches and 7 inches long
    Triangle II,   legs 8 inches and 8 inches long
    Triangle III,   legs 3 inches and 13 inches long
    Triangle IV,   legs 5 inches and 12 inches long
    Triangle V,   legs 4 inches and 16 inches long
Which of the above triangles have the SAME area?

    A. I and II   B. III and IV   C. I and V   D. II and V

5. Due to a nationwide fuel shortage, the speed limit on a major highway was lowered 5 miles per hour. Assume that a certain motorist always drives at the legal speed limit. If he were able to drive 99 miles in 2 1/5 hours at the original speed limit, how long will it take him to drive 100 miles at the new speed limit? _____ hours _____ minutes.   5._____

    A. 2; 12   B. 2; 20   C. 2; 30   D. 2; 50

6. If the pressure (P) of a gas in a closed container varies directly with the temperature (T) and inversely with the volume (V) of the container, which of the following is TRUE? If the   6._____

    A. temperature is increased, the volume is increased.
    B. pressure is decreased, the temperature is increased.
    C. volume is increased, the pressure is increased.
    D. temperature is increased, the pressure is increased.

7. A computer operator types an average of 75 lines an hour for a normal day of 7 hours. If 20% of the lines must be verified, how many of the operator's lines must be verified in a normal 5-day work week?   7._____

    A. 115   B. 263   C. 525   D. 2625

8. If the Law of Division applying to exponents states that $X^m x^n = X^{m-n}$, what does $2^6 \div 2^4$ equal?   8._____

    A. 1   B. 4   C. 8   D. 16

9. In one state, the tax rate on the purchase price of an automobile is 3% higher than the tax rate in a neighboring state. The base price of the automobile is $3000 in both states. If the automobile costs $3120 in the state with the lower tax rate, what does it cost in the state with the higher tax rate?   9._____

    A. $3120   B. $3210   C. $3300   D. $3936

10. There are 30 coins in a cash register, comprised of nickels, dimes, and quarters. If there are three times as many nickels as there are dimes, and six times as many quarters as there are dimes, what is the cash value of the total number of nickels?   10._____

    A. 15¢   B. 30¢   C. 45¢   D. 60¢

11. The formula for the circumference of all circles is $C = 2\pi r$, where r represents the radius. What is the circumference of a given circle with a diameter equal to 2π ?   11._____

    A. $2\pi^2$ B. $2\pi d$ C. $4\pi^2 r$ D. $4\pi d$

12. A saline solution contains 45 grams of salt and 255 grams of water. If 10 grams of salt are added, approximately how many grams of water must be added to bring the solution back to its original concentration?   12._____

    A. 312   B. 57   C. 35   D. 10

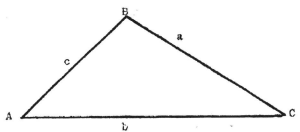

13. Let K represent the area of the above triangle ABC. K may be obtained through the use   13.____
    of the following formula $K = \sqrt{S(S-a)(S-b)(S-c)}$ where a, b, and c represent the three
    sides of triangle ABC and S = 1/2 (a+b+c). If a = 9 feet, b = 11 feet, and c = 4 feet, area K
    is MOST NEARLY equal to _____ feet.

    A. 24   B. 20   C. 17   D. 12

14. An empty tank with a total capacity of 10,000 gallons is being filled with water at the rate   14.____
    of 45 gallons a minute. However, due to a leak, the water is simultaneously flowing out of
    the tank at a rate of 200 gallons an hour.
    At the moment the tank finally holds its 10,000 gallon capacity, how many gallons of
    water will have flowed out of it due to the leak?

    A. 800   B. 740   C. 270   D. 222

15. A sorting machine can process 700 cards in one minute. If a job containing 15,000 data   15.____
    cards requires 40% of these cards to be sorted, the length of time that it will take the
    sorter to process the necessary number of cards is, MOST NEARLY, _____ minutes and
    _____ seconds.

    A. 8;34   B. 7; 57   C. 7; 14   D. 5;7

16. An operator can process 175 sheets in an hour. A laser printer can print 100 sheets a   16.____
    minute, and an optical scanner can upload 70 sheets a minute. Allowing five minutes
    between each successive operation, what is the amount of time it should take for the
    same operator to process, print and upload 1,050 cards?
    _____ hours, _____ minutes and _____ seconds.

    A. 5; 15; 50   B. 6; 35; 30
    C. 6; 50; 20   D. 7; 0; 40

17. If there are red, yellow, and green marbles in a jar, 20% of which are either red or green,   17.____
    what are the chances of blindly picking a yellow marble out of the jar? _____ out of

    _____ .

    A. 4; 5   B. 1; 3   C. 1; 5   D. 2; 3

18. There are 360 degrees in a circle, and the total area of a circle is equal to where r repre-   18.____
    sents the radius. The area of a sector of a circle is proportional to the number of degrees
    in that sector.
    The area in square inches of a sector or 45 of a circle with a radius of 4 inches is

    A. 8π   B. 8 / π   C. 16 / π   D. 2π

Questions 19 - 21.

DIRECTIONS: Answer questions 19 through 21 on the basis of the following graphs depicting various relationships in a single retail store.

Graph I

Relationship Between Number of Customers In Store And Time of Day
NO. OF CUSTOMERS

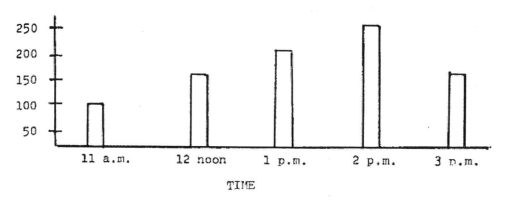

Graph II

Relationship Between Number of Check Out Lanes Available in Store And Wait Time For Check-Out

TIME IN
MINUTES

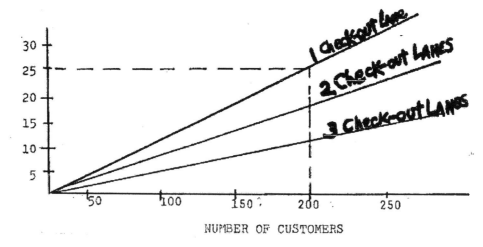

Note the dotted lines in Graph II. The demonstrate that, if there are 200 people in the store and only 1 check-out lane is open, the wait time will be 25 minutes.

19.   At what time would a person be most likely NOT to have to wait more than 15 minutes if only one check-out lane is open?   19.____

A. 11 a.m.   B. 12 noon   C. 1 p.m.   D. 3 p.m.

20. At what time of the day would a person have to wait the LONGEST to check out if 3   20.____
    check-out lanes are available?

    A. 11 a.m.   B. 12 noon   C. 1 p.m.   D. 2 p.m.

21. The difference in wait times between 1 and 3 check-out lanes at 3 p.m. is, MOST   21.____
    NEARLY,

    A. 5   B. 10   C. 15   D. 20

Questions 22 - 26.

DIRECTIONS: Answer questions 22 through 26 on the basis of the chart and the notes given
               below.

Notes:
1. Tasks 1, 2, and 3 comprise a project.
2. The horizontal line below the number given for each week represents the point at
   which the preceding week ends and the new week begins.
3. Task 2 may start only after a minimum of 2 weeks of progress has been made on
   Task 1.
4. Task 3 may start only after a minimum of 3 weeks, of work progress has been
   made on Task 2.
5. Task 1 requires 1 person. Task 2 requires 2 people. Task 3 requires 3 people.
6. Assume that all people are equally productive and that adding people to a task
   reduces the amount of time necessary to complete the task.

22. At week 4 the total number of people working on the project is   22.____

    A. 1   B. 2   C. 3   D. 4

23. Assume that Task 1 is delayed 1 week in starting. Task 2 is rescheduled but its new start   23.____
    date is delayed 2 weeks. What is the expected completion date of the project?
    Week _____ .

    A. 10   B. 11   C. 13   D. 14

24. At what week number would the project end if an additional person were added to Task 1   24.____
    at week 2?
    Week _____.

    A. 7   B. 8   C. 9   D. 10

25. If two additional people were added to Task 2, week 3, at what week number would the project end?
Week _____ .   25.____

    A. 8   B. 9   C. 10   D. 11

26. If three additional people were added to Task 3 at week 6, at what week number would the project end?
Week _____ .   26.____

    A. 6   B. 7   C. 8   D. 9

Questions 27 - 35.

DIRECTIONS: Questions 27 through 35 each consists of a series of numbers which follow in sequence according to a certain rule. Determine the rule and use it to select the next number from among the four choices given on the right side of each row. *PRINT THE LETTER OF THE CORRECT ANSWER IN THE SPACE AT THE RIGHT.*

        SAMPLE X: 3   .6 9   12   15   18

        A. 19   B. 20   C. 21   D. 22

In sample X above, the rule is to add 3 to each successive number in the series in order to get the next number. Therefore, since 18 plus 3 is 21, the correct choice is C.

        SAMPLE Y: 4   6 9   13   18   24

        A. 27   B. 28   C. 29   D. 31

In sample Y above, the rule is to add 2, then add 3, then add 4, etc., to each successive number in the series to get the next number. Therefore, the correct choice is D.

27. 3   9   4   12 7   21   27.____
    A. 25   B. 18   C. 16   D. 8

28. 5   3   6   3   9   5   28.____
    A. 20   B. 18   C. 10   D. 3

29. 10 8   12 4   20 -12   29.____
    A. 52   B. 48   C. 0   D. -26

30. 3   10 9   15 13 18   30.____
    A. 12   B. 15   C. 20   D. 36

31. 1   1   3   9   13 65   31.____
    A. 15   B. 26   C. 71   D. 102

32. 2   6   5   15 13 39   32.____
    A. 4   B. 18   C. 36   D. 39

33. 48 8   40 10 30 15   33.____

    A. 15   B. 20   C. 25   D. 42

34. 20 5   30 10 50 25   34.____

    A. 110   B. 100   C. 75   D. 40

35. 4   24 12 60 20 80   35.____

    A. 40   B. 36   C. 20   D. 8

KEY (CORRECT ANSWERS)

1.	A	11.	A	21.	B	31.	C
2.	A	12.	B	22.	C	32.	C
3.	D	13.	C	23.	C	33.	A
4.	D	14.	A	24.	D	34.	B
5.	C	15.	A	25.	B	35.	C
6.	D	16.	B	26.	C		
7.	C	17.	A	27.	C		
8.	B	18.	D	28.	A		
9.	B	19.	A	29.	A		
10.	C	20.	D	30.	B		

EXAMINATION SECTION
TEST 1

DIRECTIONS: Each question or incomplete statement is followed by several suggested answers or completions. Select the one the BEST answers the question or completes the statement. *PRINT THE LETTER OF THE CORRECT ANSWER IN THE SPACE AT THE RIGHT.*

1. Which of the following was an advantage associated with open source software in the 1990s?

   A. A standard user interface for productivity applications such as word processing and spreadsheets
   B. Stringent quality control processes
   C. Suitability for mission-critical applications
   D. A broadened community of programmers who can stabilize and add functionality to software

1._____

2. IP addresses
   I. are attached to every node on the Internet
   II. are sometimes listed as a character string
   III. establish a direct link between sender and recipient
   IV. use circuit-switching technology

   A. I only
   B. I and II
   C. II, III and IV
   D. I, II, III and IV

2._____

3. Programming languages used exclusively for artificial intelligence applications include

   A. AIML and Prolog
   B. LISP and Prolog
   C. Ada and LISP
   D. Delphi and Python

3._____

4. Cookies are usually stored by browsers as

   A. text files
   B. algorithms
   C. tokens
   D. HTML files

4._____

5. Analysts typically use each of the following to evaluate the flow of data through an information system, EXCEPT

   A. decision trees
   B. Gantt charts
   C. structured English
   D. data flow diagrams

5._____

6. Methods for protecting a computer system from viruses include
   I. accessing a Web site that offers on-line virus scans

6._____

    II.   checking physical media, such as floppy disks or DVDs, before they are used in a computer

    III.   erecting a firewall

    IV.   never opening e-mail attachments from people unknown to the user

    A.   I and IV
    B.   II, III and IV
    C.   III and IV only
    D.   I, II, III and IV

7.   Describing an algorithm as "general" means that it   7._____

    A.   does not have a clear stopping point
    B.   addresses the stated problem in all instances
    C.   can be carried out in any sequence
    D.   can be expressed in any language

8.   Packet-switching offers each of the following advantages, EXCEPT   8._____

    A.   faster transmission of data
    B.   greater network user capacity
    C.   greater degree of redundancy
    D.   more localized data corruption

9.   The term "digital divide" describes the discrepancies between   9._____

    A.   people who have access to, and the resources to use, new information and communication technologies, and people who do not
    B.   approximations in the values of floating-point numbers by a processor
    C.   the rate at which computer processing speeds increase and the rate at which the capacity to store data increases
    D.   data that is entered into a database application and the information that is displayed to an end-user

10. The main advantage of using programmable microcode is that   10._____

    A.   programs can be made very small and portable
    B.   the CPU's capacity is never overclocked
    C.   the same instructions can be executed on different hardware platforms
    D.   it is usually executed more quickly than other program code

11. Cache memory is NOT   11._____

    A.   used only in large computers
    B.   used to solve the problem of inadequate primary memory
    C.   divided into the two main categories of RAM cache and secondary cache
    D.   used to improve processing speed

12. When PC users ask for a document to be sent to them, they should request a .txt file, because it   12._____

    A.   comes with a built-in antivirus program
    B.   will only transmit text

C.   denotes a disinfected file
D.   cannot contain malicious and executable code

13.   Line personnel in an organization can enter transaction data and see totals and other   13.____
      results immediately by use of _____ processing

      A.   summary
      B.   batch
      C.   on-line
      D.   real-time

14.   A network with a main computer that does all of the processing for a number of simple   14.____
      display units is described as

      A.   peer-to-peer
      B.   client-file server
      C.   n-tier
      D.   terminal emulation

15.   All buses consist of two parts, the _____ bus and the _____ bus.   15.____

      A.   internal; external
      B.   main; expansion
      C.   ISA; PCI
      D.   address; data

16.   The _____ is a small amount of high-speed memory thatstores regularly used data.   16.____

      A.   cache
      B.   spool
      C.   buffer
      D.   frame

17.   Technological cornerstones of the Internet include each of the following, EXCEPT   17.____

      A.   HTML
      B.   TCP/IP
      C.   URL
      D.   MMDS

18.   The OSI (Open System Interconnection) model defines a networking framework for   18.____
      implementing protocols in seven layers. The _____ layer, or layer 3, provides switching
      and routing technologies, creating logical paths, known as virtual circuits, for transmitting
      data from node to node

      A.   network
      B.   presentation
      C.   transport
      D.   session

19. The main difference between the Windows NT operating system and the current Windows OS is that the NT operating system

    A. has no relationship to MS-DOS
    B. has a different user interface
    C. runs faster
    D. supports more peripheral devices

19.____

20. Before sound can be handled on a computer, it must first be converted to electrical energy, and then transformed through an analog-to-digital converter into a digital representation. _____ Law states that the more often a sound wave is sampled, the more accurate the digital representation.

    A. Gilder's
    B. Moore's
    C. Amdahl's
    D. Nyquist's

20.____

21. The primary disadvantage associated with interpreted programming languages, such as Java, is that they

    A. present fewer solutions to individual problems
    B. have slower execution speeds
    C. are not as portable
    D. are more difficult for programmers to understand

21.____

22. The advantages promised by the emerging technology of holographic storage include
    I.   higher storage densities
    II. easier synchronization with the CPU
    III. non-volatility
    IV. faster data transfer speeds

    A. I only
    B. I and IV
    C. II and III
    D. III and IV

22.____

23. A file that contains instructions in a particular computer's machine language is said to contain _____ code.

    A. macro
    B. object
    C. scripting
    D. source

23.____

24. A computer uses _____ to transform raw data into useful information.

    A. input devices and output devices
    B. a processor and memory
    C. memory and a motherboard
    D. language and protocols

24.____

42

25. In computer graphics, the term "raster graphics" is synonymous with   25.____

    A. vector graphics
    B. bitmapped graphics
    C. object-oriented graphics
    D. autosizing

26. In 1996, journalist and former White House Press Secretary Pierre Salinger, making a   26.____
public statement about the causes of the recent TWA Flight 800 crash, became the fig-
urehead for what is now known as the "Pierre Salinger Syndrome" This phenomenon
refers to the

    A. act of hiding information by embedding messages within another
    B. pit those who have the skills, knowledge and abilities to use the technologies
       against those who do not
    C. tendency to believe that everything one reads on the Internet is true
    D. practice of using software to monitor the behavior of a user visiting a Web site or
       sending an e-mail

27. Which of the following is NOT a term that is interchangeable with "expansion card"?   27.____

    A. Expansion file
    B. Expansion board
    C. Adapter
    D. Socket

28. Multidimensional database management systems are also referred to as   28.____

    A. Relational database management systems
    B. On-line Transaction Processing (OLTP)
    C. SQL servers
    D. On-line Analytical Processing (OLAP)

29. The primary difference between "smart" and "dumb" printers is that   29.____

    A. smart printers can perform dithering
    B. smart printers use a page description language
    C. dumb printers use less system memory
    D. dumb printers cannot bitmap vector graphics

30. The interface between the CPU and the hard disk's electronics is known as the hard disk   30.____

    A. navigator
    B. manager
    C. reticulate
    D. controller

31. A single _____ port can be used to connect as many as 127 peripheral devices to a   31.____
computer.

    A. PIA
    B. Fire Wire
    C. parallel
    D. USB

32. In the binary system, 1011 equals a decimal   32.____

    A. 2
    B. 3
    C. 11
    D. 12

33. A transistor radio is an example of _____ transmission of data   33.____

    A. half-duplex
    B. full-duplex
    C. half-simplex
    D. simplex

34. Which of the following is NOT a type of liquid crystal display?   34.____

    A. Active matrix
    B. Passive matrix
    C. Electroluminescent
    D. Dual-scan

35. Which of the following is a term for commercial software that has been pirated and made   35.____
available to the public via a bulletin board system (BBS) or the Internet?

    A. Freeware
    B. Crackware
    C. Warez
    D. Shareware

36. IBM-compatible PCs denote the primary hard disk with the   36.____

    A. number 1
    B. letter A
    C. letter C
    D. letter X

37. Each of the following operating systems provides some kind of graphical user interface,   37.____
EXCEPT

    A. Macintosh OS
    B. Linux
    C. UNIX
    D. DOS

38. An operating system's overall quality is most often judged on its ability to manage   38.____

    A. program execution
    B. device drivers
    C. disk utilities
    D. application backup

39. In multimedia product development, elements of a program are arranged into separate   39.____

    A. tracks
    B. columns

C. zones
D. layers

40. The CPU contains the _____ unit.   40._____
    I. I/O
    II. control
    III. arithmetic
    IV. instructing decoding

    A. I and II
    B. I, II and IV
    C. II and V
    D. I, II, III and IV

41. The on-line application that locates and displays the document associated with a hyper-   41._____
    link is a(n)

    A. server
    B. plug-in
    C. browser
    D. finder

42. Which of the following devices requires a driver?   42._____
    I. printer
    II. mouse
    III. DVD drive
    IV. keyboard

    A. I only
    B. I, II and IV
    C. II and IV
    D. I,II, III and IV

43. Database management systems include each of the following components, EXCEPT   43._____

    A. data collection applications
    B. statistical analysis applications
    C. data modification applications
    D. query languages

44. Waves are characterized by each of the following, EXCEPT   44._____

    A. Frequency
    B. Pulse
    C. Frequency
    D. Amplitude

45. Although considered to be outdated by many programmers, _____ is still the most   45._____
    widely used programming language in the world.

    A. Pascal
    B. COBOL
    C. FORTRAN
    D. BASIC

46. A graphics program using the _____ model represents three-dimensional objects by displaying their outlines and edges.

    A. wireframe
    B. volumetric
    C. solid
    D. surface

46._____

47. The concept central to the legislation that regulates telephone service in the United States is

    A. broadband service
    B. consumer price parity
    C. reasonable access time
    D. universal access

47._____

48. In order to be certified as "open source" by the Open Source Institute (OSI), a program must meet each of the following criteria, EXCEPT that the

    A. rights attached to the program are contingent on the program's being part of a particular software distribution
    B. author or holder of the license of the source code cannot collect royalties on the distribution of the program
    C. distributed program must make the source code accessible to the user
    D. licensed software cannot place restrictions on other software distributed with it

48._____

49. Ethernet systems typically use a _____ topology.

    A. bus
    B. star
    C. ring
    D. tree

49._____

50. In enterprises, the _____ is the computer that routes the traffic from a workstation to the outside network that is serving the Web pages.

    A. proxy server
    B. ISP
    C. packet switcher
    D. gateway

50._____

KEY (CORRECT ANSWERS)

1.	D	11.	A	21.	B	31.	D	41.	C
2.	B	12.	D	22.	B	32.	C	42.	D
3.	B	13.	C	23.	B	33.	D	43.	A
4.	A	14.	A	24.	B	34.	C	44.	B
5.	B	15.	D	25.	B	35.	C	45.	B
6.	D	16.	A	26.	C	36.	C	46.	A
7.	B	17.	D	27.	D	37.	D	47.	D
8.	A	18.	A	28.	D	38.	A	48.	A
9.	A	19.	A	29.	B	39.	A	49.	A
10.	C	20.	D	30.	D	40.	B	50.	D

TEST 2

DIRECTIONS: Each question or incomplete statement is followed by several suggested answers or completions. Select the one the BEST answers the question or completes the statement. *PRINT THE LETTER OF THE CORRECT ANSWER IN THE SPACE AT THE RIGHT.*

1. "Refresh rate" typically refers to the

   A. number of times RAM is updated in a second
   B. time it takes to completely rewrite a disk
   C. number of times the display monitor is redrawn in a second
   D. time it takes for a Web pages to reload

   1.____

2. In a markup language, authors use _____ to identify portions of a document.

   A. icons
   B. schemas
   C. numbers
   D. elements

   2.____

3. Object-oriented programming languages rely heavily on _____ to create high-level objects.

   I. formalization
   II. abstraction
   III. information hiding
   IV. encapsulation

   A. I only
   B. I, II and III
   C. II, III and IV
   D. I, II, III and IV

   3.____

4. The base unit of three-dimensional graphics is the

   A. texel
   B. voxel
   C. pixel
   D. bit

   4.____

5. In computing, "gamma correction" typically refers to an adjustment in the

   A. light intensity of a scanner, monitor, or printer
   B. amplitude modulation
   C. emission of gamma waves by a CRT monitor
   D. speed with which analog data is digitized

   5.____

6. The OSI (Open System Interconnection) model defines a networking framework for implementing protocols in seven layers. The seventh layer of the OSI model consists of the

   A. hardware
   B. applications

   6.____

C. protocols
D. network

7. A significant difference between frame switching packet switching is that frame switching 7.____

A. offers accelerated packet processing
B. creates a virtual circuit
C. allows multiple connections on the same set of hardware
D. contains now quality-of-service assurances

8. In _____ memory, each location has an actual "address." 8.____

A. RAM
B. ROM
C. PROM
D. EPROM

9. Video applications require a bare minimum of _____ frames per second in order to function. 9.____

A. 8
B. 15
C. 30
D. 60

10. The most commonly used network application today is 10.____

A. Web design
B. BBS
C. e-mail
D. software downloading

11. Standardized codes for representing character data numerically include 11.____
    I. ANSI
    II. EBCDIC
    III. ASCII
    IV. DECS

A. I and II
B. II and III
C. II, III and IV
D. I, II, III and IV

12. Photolithography is the process of transferring geometric shapes on a mask to the surface of a silicon wafer. Possible future alternative technologies to photolithography include each of the following, EXCEPT the 12.____

A. multiple-wave laser beam
B. electron beam
C. extreme ultraviolet
D. X-ray

13. Hard disk mechanisms typically contain a single

    A. head actuator
    B. read/write head
    C. platter
    D. landing zone

14. Contemporary Rapid Application Development (RAD) emphasizes the reduction of development time through

    A. trimming code
    B. inserting pre-written artificial intelligence capabilities
    C. establishing a graphical user interface
    D. making slight modifications to proprietary software

15. A Web site contains a number of databases that contain all the information about an organization's clients-such as names, addresses, credit card information, past invoices, etc.). This is an example of a data

    A. mine
    B. warehouse
    C. dictionary
    D. mart

16. Currently, a computer's most difficult task would be to

    A. speak in long paragraphs
    B. recognize spoken words
    C. interpret the meaning of words
    D. compose a syntactically correct item of discourse

17. An API is a(n)

    A. algorithm for the lossless compression of files
    B. set of routines, protocols, and tools for building software applications
    C. piece of software that helps the operating system communicate with a peripheral device
    D. code for representing characters as numbers

18. The disadvantages associated with ring LAN topologies include
    I. more limited geographical range
    II. low bandwidth
    III. high expense
    IV. complex and difficult installation

    A. I only
    B. I and II
    C. III and IV
    D. I, II, III and IV

19. Scientists would most likely use _____ to analyze variations in planetary orbits.

    A. a mainframe
    B. the Internet

C. a supercomputer
D. a virtual network

20. The primary disadvantage to shared-memory multiprocessing involves   20._____

    A. slow retrieval speeds
    B. bus overload
    C. inadequate trace width
    D. RAM purges

21. If a computer user enters a legal command that does not make any sense in the given   21._____
context, the user has committed an error of

    A. syntax
    B. semantics
    C. formatting
    D. parsing

22. Which of the following terms is NOT synonymous with the others?   22._____

    A. Floating point unit
    B. Numeric coprocessor
    C. Math coprocessor
    D. Accelerator board

23. Which of the following is a measure of data transfer capacity?   23._____

    A. Duplication rate
    B. Bandwidth
    C. Frequency
    D. Baud rate

24. In the 1990s, the main obstacle to the use of the Linux operating system in desktop appli-   24._____
cations was

    A. the lack of a standard user interface
    B. difficulties in file and print serving
    C. inability to accommodate multiple platforms
    D. insufficient support from the commercial sector

25. Which of the following external bus standards supports "hot plugging"–the ability to add   25._____
and remove devices to a computer while the computer is running and have the operating
system automatically recognize the change?

    A. Serial
    B. USB
    C. PCI
    D. Parallel port

26. When a key on a computer keyboard is struck, each of the following may occur, EXCEPT   26._____

    A. a cursor on the screen moves
    B. a scan code is sent to an application

C. a binary number is input into the computer
D. an EBCDIC code for a letter is sent to a word processing application

27. SONET   27.____

A. cannot be used to link digital networks to fiber optics
B. is a synchronous Layer 1 protocol
C. prohibits data streams of different speeds from being multiplexed in the same line
D. can scale up to 4 Gbps

28. A user handles data stored on a disk with the utility program known as the   28.____

A. file sorter
B. file manager
C. disk scanner
D. finder

29. A _____ is a tool that helps users of word processing or desktop publishing applications   29.____
to avoid formatting complex documents individually.

A. merge
B. column
C. template
D. table

30. Which of the following is a high-level programming language that is particularly suited for   30.____
use on the World Wide Web, often through the use of small, downloadable applications
known as applets?

A. XML
B. Ada
C. Java
D. C++

31. Microprocessor speeds have increased dramatically over the past two decades, largely   31.____
as a result of significant

A. improvements in hardware breakpoints
B. increases in trace depth
C. compression of overlay RAM
D. reductions in trace width

32. On most PCs, this contains all the code required to control the keyboard, display screen,   32.____
disk drives, serial communications, and a number of miscellaneous functions.

A. Flash memory
B. Operating system
C. BIOS
D. USB

33. Which of the following is a rating system originally designed to help parents and teachers control what children access on the Internet, but now also used to facilitate other uses for labels, including code signing and privacy?   33.____

   A. V-chip
   B. Recreational Software Advisory Council
   C. Platform for Internet Content Selection
   D. Cyber Patrol

34. A database designed for continuous addition and deletion of records is said to perform the function of _____ processing.   34.____

   A. batch
   B. drilldown
   C. transaction
   D. analytical

35. A unique 128-bit number, produced by the Windows OS or by some Windows applications to identify a particular component, application, file, database entry, and/or user is known as a   35.____

   A. key
   B. GUID
   C. PGP
   D. DLL

36. Compared to private-key cryptograph, public-key   36.____

   A. uses two keys
   B. is easier to understand
   C. functions more smoothly with contemporary networks
   D. requires fewer computations

37. Static RAM (SRAM) is used to   37.____

   A. supplement the main memory
   B. determine which information should be kept in the cache
   C. form the memory cache
   D. form the disk cache

38. A(n) _____ system is used to produce reports that will help managers throughout an organization to evaluate their departments.   38.____

   A. expert
   B. management information
   C. office automation
   D. transaction processing

39. Software that may be delivered/downloaded and used without charge, but is nevertheless still copyrighted by the author, is known as   39.____

   A. public-domain software
   B. shareware

C. open-source software
D. freeware

40. Barriers to widespread use of cable modems in Internet access include   40._____
      I. the one-way transmission design of the television infrastructure
      II. uncertain capacity of television infrastructure
      III. complexity of protocols
      IV. bandwidth restrictions

    A. I only
    B. I and II
    C. II and IV
    D. I, II, III and IV

41. Which of the following is NOT a function that can be performed with a spreadsheet appli-   41._____
cation?

    A. Budget charts and graphs
    B. Inventory management
    C. Audiovisual presentations
    D. Fiscal forecasting

42. Which of the following is a Windows-based graphical user interface for the UNIX operat-   42._____
ing system?

    A. Linux
    B. Gnu
    C. MOTIF
    D. UNI

43. In a database, the _____ contains a code, number, name, or some other information   43._____
that uniquely identifies the record.

    A. primary key
    B. file
    C. schema
    D. key field

44. Which of the following terms is NOT synonymous with the others?   44._____

    A. Web bug
    B. Clear GIF
    C. Web beacon
    D. Cookie

45. As a firewall technology, the proxy server operates by   45._____

    A. examining each packet that enters or exits a network, and accepts or rejects it
       based on a given set of rules
    B. applying security mechanisms to specific applications
    C. constantly changing its location
    D. intercepting all messages entering and leaving a network

46. VRAM is a specific kind of memory used to   46._____

    A. accelerate processing speeds
    B. store video display data
    C. create virtual addresses, rather than real addresses, to store data and instructions
    D. create a virtual environment for the user

47. Which phase of the application development process serves to identify features that   47._____
must be added to the program to make it satisfactory to users?

    A. Software concept
    B. Coding and debugging
    C. System testing
    D. Requirements analysis

48. What is the term for the natural data size of a computer?   48._____

    A. Word size
    B. Clock speed
    C. Bus width
    D. Cache

49. Microkernels operate by moving many of the operating system services into "user space"   49._____
that other operating systems keep in the kernel. This migration tends to have each of the
following effects, EXCEPT greater

    A. security
    B. bug immunity for the kernel
    C. configurability
    D. "fixed" memory footprint

50. High-level programming languages are   50._____
    I. useful when speed is essential
    II. processor-independent
    III. usually compiled or assembled
    IV. easier to read, write and maintain than other languages

    A. I and IV
    B. I, II, and III
    C. II, III and IV
    D. I, II, III and IV

KEY (CORRECT ANSWERS)

1.	C	11.	C	21.	B	31.	D	41.	C
2.	D	12.	A	22.	D	32.	C	42.	C
3.	C	13.	A	23.	B	33.	C	43.	A
4.	A	14.	C	24.	A	34.	C	44.	D
5.	A	15.	B	25.	B	35.	B	45.	D
6.	B	16.	C	26.	D	36.	A	46.	B
7.	B	17.	B	27.	B	37.	C	47.	C
8.	A	18.	C	28.	B	38.	B	48.	A
9.	B	19.	C	29.	C	39.	C	49.	D
10.	C	20.	B	30.	C	40.	B	50.	C

EXAMINATION SECTION
TEST 1

DIRECTIONS: Each question or incomplete statement is followed by several suggested answers or completions. Select the one that BEST answers the question or completes the statement. *PRINT THE LETTER OF THE CORRECT ANSWER IN THE SPACE AT THE RIGHT.*

1. Knowledge work systems are most typically used by each of the following personnel EXCEPT

    A. middle managers   B. salespeople
    C. engineers   D. accountants

1.____

2. A media-oriented description of a system's operations is BEST represented by a(n)

    A. systems flowchart   B. system requirements plan
    C. Gantt chart   D. program flowchart

2.____

3. During preliminary analysis, a feasibility group will study the three fundamental operations of an existing system.
Which of the following is NOT one of these operations?

    A. Output of information
    B. Data processing
    C. Coding
    D. Data preparation and input

3.____

4. Normally, the starting point of any systems design is to determine the

    A. output   B. hardware
    C. throughput   D. users

4.____

5. From its beginnings, the total time required for an entire systems analysis and design process to be completed will MOST likely be

    A. 6-12 months   B. 12-18 months
    C. 2-3 years   D. 3-5 years

5.____

6. In a data flow diagram, a square like the one shown at the right would be used to represent

    A. input to the system   B. a terminal
    C. magnetic tape   D. a display

6.____

7. A _____ systems conversion takes place when the old system is switched off and the new one is started up.

    A. day-one   B. direct   C. parallel   D. pilot

7.____

8. The MOST common reason for the failure of an information system is

    A. faulty programming
    B. hardware obsolescence
    C. interface complications
    D. faulty problem identification

8.____

9. A personnel record in a master file consists of the following fields, containing the indicated number of characters.

Field	Number of Characters
Identication number	5
Social Security number	9
Name	25
Address	35
Sex	2
Code number	1

If the master file contains 2,000 transactions, then approximately how many characters would the file be expected to hold?

A. 56,000   B. 115,500   C. 154,000   D. 231,000

10. Which of the following is NOT one of the primary elements of a data flow diagram?

A. Process   B. External entity
C. Rule number   D. Data store

11. During systems design, each of the following is a consideration involving input EXCEPT

A. media   B. validity checking
C. volume   D. security

12. The MAIN advantage involved with the use of pilot systems conversion is

A. speed of conversion process
B. provides constant backup media
C. makes file conversion unnecessary
D. minimizes problems by confining operations

13. _____ is NOT a type of systems control.

A. Auditing   B. Contingency planning
C. Data security   D. Data control

14. In a _____ type of systems conversion, various capabilities are added to the system over a number of years.

A. graduated   B. pilot   C. phased   D. indirect

15. Which of the following is NOT a standard classification for a system in terms of cost-effectiveness?

A. Risky   B. Safe
C. Pioneering   D. Prudent

16. _____ accounts for the GREATEST expenditure involved in the cost of creating and maintaining a system.

A. Systems design
B. Equipment
C. Evaluation and maintenance
D. Implementation

17. Which of the following is NOT one of the procedures involved in program development?   17._____

    A. Program preparation   B. Systems audit evaluation
    C. Scheduling   D. Testing

18. The PRIMARY purpose of the systems analysis phase of the entire analysis and design   18._____
    process is to

    A. compose an accurate data flow diagram
    B. determine input, output, and processing requirements
    C. determine whether to modify the existing system or convert completely to a new
       one
    D. consider the people who will be interacting with the new system

19. Which of the following is NOT a major problem associated with systems building?   19._____

    A. Coordination costs   B. Hardware currency
    C. Requirements analysis   D. Record keeping

20. Typically, a workable system is the output of the _____ phase of systems analysis and   20._____
    design.

    A. systems development   B. systems analysis
    C. systems design   D. implementation

21. The MOST reliable means of obtaining information about an existing system can be   21._____
    obtained through the use of

    A. observations   B. personal interviews
    C. questionnaires   D. written forms

22. The purpose of a printer spacing chart is to   22._____

    A. represent the exact format of a system's output
    B. assist in data validity checking
    C. coordinate all related fields into a single report
    D. describe the input data needed to produce the system's output

23. The FIRST procedure in a system test plan is usually _____ testing.   23._____

    A. crash proof   B. system
    C. personnel   D. unit

24. The cost-benefit analysis of a proposed system is USUALLY performed during the   24._____
    _____ phase of analysis and design.

    A. systems design   B. systems analysis
    C. preliminary analysis   D. implementation

25. The MOST significant output of the systems analysis phase of the entire analysis and   25._____
    design process is the

    A. detailed system design
    B. system requirements plan
    C. installed and operational system
    D. preliminary plan

KEY (CORRECT ANSWERS)

1.	B	11.	D
2.	A	12.	D
3.	C	13.	A
4.	A	14.	C
5.	C	15.	A
6.	A	16.	D
7.	B	17.	B
8.	D	18.	C
9.	C	19.	B
10.	C	20.	A

21.	B
22.	A
23.	D
24.	A
25.	B

TEST 2

DIRECTIONS: Each question or incomplete statement is followed by several suggested answers or completions. Select the one that BEST answers the question or completes the statement. *PRINT THE LETTER OF THE CORRECT ANSWER IN THE SPACE AT THE RIGHT.*

1. Systems maintenance involves three important factors that are considered during the design and development phases of a project. Which of the following is NOT one of these three?

    A. Structured programming
    B. System documentation
    C. System auditing
    D. Anticipation of future needs

    1._____

2. In a data flow diagram, an open-ended rectangle like the one shown at the right would be used to represent

    A. an invoice
    B. a punched card
    C. data storage
    D. data preparation

    2._____

3. Systems design reports normally include each of the following EXCEPT a(n)

    A. review of the problems associated with the present system
    B. overview of the proposed system
    C. summation of the major findings of the cost-benefit analysis
    D. list of hardware recommended for the proposed system

    3._____

4. A _____ group is NOT usually involved in a typical systems project team.

    A. vendor
    B. user
    C. management
    D. programming

    4._____

5. The _____ method of systems conversion is typically the riskiest.

    A. parallel   B. pilot   C. day-one   D. direct

    5._____

6. The PRIMARY purpose of a decision table used in systems analysis is to

    A. describe the sequence of operations that must be performed to obtain a computer solution to a problem
    B. represent all the combinations of conditions that must be satisfied before an action can be taken
    C. describe the operations to be performed by the system, with a major emphasis on the media involved, as well as the workstations through which they pass
    D. graphically depict the flow of data and the processes that change or transform data throughout the system

    6._____

7. Which of the following is used to describe a system's necessary input data?

    A. Systems flowchart
    B. CRT layout form
    C. Data flow diagram
    D. Record layout form

    7._____

8. The LONGEST phase involved in the systems analysis and design process is the
   _____ phase.

   8._____

   A. implementation   B. systems design
   C. systems development   D. preliminary analysis

9. The systems development phase of analysis and design normally includes each of the
   following EXCEPT

   9._____

   A. purchase of equipment   B. program testing
   C. user training   D. program development

10. In cases where it is too expensive to convert a system's old files and applications, a(n)
    _____ system conversion is commonly used.

    10._____

    A. parallel   B. pilot   C. direct   D. day-one

11. The PRIMARY purpose of an audit trail is to

    11._____

    A. trace specific input data to its related output
    B. error-check a new systems program
    C. locate workstations where unauthorized users are at work
    D. check data validity

12. A system requirements plan typically includes each of the following EXCEPT

    12._____

    A. description of how existing system works
    B. hardware requirements for the new system
    C. information necessary for the new system
    D. major problems of existing system

13. A _____ is typically a member of the programming group of a systems project team.

    13._____

    A. vendor   B. user
    C. management   D. librarian

14. The implementation phase of systems analysis and design does NOT usually include

    14._____

    A. training   B. auditing
    C. programming   D. system conversion

15. The _____ is a document created by the systems project team that takes into account
    the organizational constraints and the personnel involved in using a new system.

    15._____

    A. system requirements report
    B. statement of objectives
    C. test plan
    D. request for proposal

16. Which of the following is used as an aid to scheduling system operations?

    16._____

    A. Gantt chart   B. Circle graph
    C. Chief programmer D. Head node

17. The MAIN disadvantage associated with parallel systems conversion is that 17.____

    A. it usually takes more time than all other approaches
    B. there is costly duplication of personnel efforts and equipment
    C. confusion is involved in constant switch-overs
    D. no backup is provided

18. Transaction processing systems are LEAST likely to be used by 18.____

    A. knowledge professionals
    B. data entry specialists
    C. customers
    D. clerks

19. When a new system is used in its entirety only in one locality or area, _____ is being practiced. 19.____

    A. batch processing   B. live data analysis
    C. pilot conversion   D. file conversion

20. Which of the following is NOT a software tool that has been developed to help a systems analyst build better systems in a more timely and cost-effective manner? 20.____

    A. CAD tools   B. Project management tools
    C. Prototyping   D. CASE tools

21. Action stubs and conditions entries are components of the 21.____

    A. program flowchart   B. decision table
    C. system flowchart   D. Gantt chart

22. When both an old and a new system are run simultaneously for a period of time to ensure the new system's proper operation, _____ is being practiced. 22.____

    A. incremental auditing   B. file conversion
    C. parallel conversion   D. direct switch-over

23. The FIRST operation performed during the implementation phase of analysis and design is usually 23.____

    A. file conversion   B. systems evaluation
    C. systems conversion   D. auditing

24. Typically, programming accounts for _____% of the hours spent on systems analysis and design. 24.____

    A. 10   B. 20   C. 35   D. 45

25. In a data flow diagram, a circle like the one shown at the right would be used to represent 25.____

    A. output from the system
    B. a single file
    C. a manual action
    D. a process that transforms data in some way

KEY (CORRECT ANSWERS)

1.	C	11.	A
2.	C	12.	B
3.	D	13.	D
4.	A	14.	C
5.	D	15.	B
6.	B	16.	A
7.	D	17.	B
8.	C	18.	A
9.	C	19.	C
10.	D	20.	A

21.	B
22.	C
23.	A
24.	B
25.	D

EXAMINATION SECTION
TEST 1

DIRECTIONS: Each question or incomplete statement is followed by several suggested answers or completions. Select the one that BEST answers the question or completes the statement. *PRINT THE LETTER OF THE CORRECT ANSWER IN THE SPACE AT THE RIGHT.*

1. The purpose of the _____ module is to show the overall flow of data through a program.   1._____

    A. file maintenance   B. read
    C. control   D. init

2. An index file consists of the _____ fields.   2._____

    A. key and record number
    B. name and masterfile
    C. date and counter
    D. record number and data address

3. Which of the following is/are used to specify detailed computer operations to implement functions?   3._____

    A. Pseudocode   B. Structure charts
    C. Data flow charts   D. Modules

4. The purpose of programming an array into an information system is to allow the user to   4._____

    A. practice random file access
    B. sequentially update files
    C. store several values for the same variable in the internal memory of the computer
    D. access any number of variables without having to script

5. What is the MOST commonly used logic structure in systems programming?   5._____

    A. Decision   B. Sequential
    C. Case   D. Loop

6. The _____ module enters data into a program.   6._____

    A. init   B. read   C. control   D. write

7. Control-break modules serve to _____ in systems programming.   7._____

    A. interrupt processing in case of a logic error
    B. transfer data from one processing path to another
    C. interrupt processing in case of a data error
    D. give subtotals for a group of similar records

8. The normal order in which modules are presented to the computer and activated are called   8._____

    A. repetitions   B. selections
    C. sequences   D. case constructs

9. The EASIEST to program is the 9.____

    A. bubble sort   B. binary search
    C. sequential search   D. merge of two lists

10. The instruction to increment a variable by one would be written 10.____

    A. COUNTER = COUNTER + 1   B. SUM = COUNTER + 1
    C. COUNTER = SUM + 1   D. SUM = SUM + VARIABLE

11. A programmer should create a(n) _____ file for storing completed file updates. 11.____

    A. transaction   B. activity
    C. backup   D. temporary

12. For the purpose of data validation, a new module will need to be processed from the _____ module. 12.____

    A. READ   B. WRAPUP   C. CALC   D. WRITE

13. A _____ module is NOT a type of process data module. 13.____

    A. control   B. print
    C. calculation   D. read

14. In a written computer solution or program flowchart, a marker is used to indicate that there are no more records to be processed.
This marker is 14.____

    A. EXIT   B. HF   C. EOF   D. END

15. The PRIMARY reason negative logic is used in systems programming is to 15.____

    A. provide a way of thinking that is more convenient for people
    B. provide a means for checking data validity
    C. increase the number of variables
    D. decrease the number of tests

16. When creating a random-access information system, a programmer sometimes *chains* modules on top of each other. The purpose of this is to 16.____

    A. make the program more interactive
    B. place data in intermediate storage of input and output, to speed up processing
    C. enable the user to use larger programs, and leave more room for data in the internal memory
    D. process all the necessary tasks after files have been updated and processed

17. An information system is programmed to put a mailing list into both alphabetical and zip code order.
What type of logic structure will be used to program the system? 17.____

    A. Decision   B. Case
    C. Sequential   D. Loop

18. Which of the following is BASIC code used to disassociate a data file from a program? 18.____

    A. END   B. DATA   C. CLOSE   D. DIM

19. Which of the following is used to load an array?   19.____

    A. WRITE module   B. Loop
    C. String   D. Primer read

20. Which of the following is NOT a type of decision logic used in the programming struc-   20.____
ture?

    A. True   B. False
    C. Conditional   D. Straight-through

21. _____ are tools primarily of the case logic structure.   21.____

    A. Decision tables   B. Codes
    C. READ modules   D. Variables

22. What type of operator, within an expression or equation, uses numerical or string data as   22.____
operands, and produces logical data as the resultant?

    A. Relational   B. Network
    C. Logical   D. Hierarchical

23. In a program flowchart, an assignment instruction would be written   23.____

    A. LET   B. VARIABLE=
    C. READ   D. WRITE AS

24. When a programmer wants the value in one array to point to an element in another array,   24.____
he uses

    A. a null file   B. a primer read
    C. a nested loop   D. the pointer technique

25. The purpose of _____ is to eliminate rewriting of identical system processes.   25.____

    A. pseudocode   B. sequences
    C. repetitions   D. modules

KEY (CORRECT ANSWERS)

1.	C		11.	B
2.	A		12.	A
3.	A		13.	A
4.	C		14.	C
5.	B		15.	D
6.	B		16.	C
7.	D		17.	D
8.	C		18.	C
9.	C		19.	B
10.	A		20.	C

21.	B
22.	A
23.	B
24.	D
25.	D

TEST 2

DIRECTIONS: Each question or incomplete statement is followed by several suggested answers or completions. Select the one that BEST answers the question or completes the statement. *PRINT THE LETTER OF THE CORRECT ANSWER IN THE SPACE AT THE RIGHT.*

1. What is the term for the summation of values within nonsignificant data fields, such as keys and identification number fields?   1.____

   A. Accumulation   B. Hash total
   C. Null files   D. Entry key total

2. The PRIMARY purpose of indicators is to   2.____

   A. maintain the processing of a loop structure
   B. change the processing path
   C. assist in nesting loops or decisions
   D. assist in detecting logic errors

3. Which of the following is NOT a means of converting positive logic to negative logic?   3.____

   A. Changing all <= to >
   B. Changing all < to >
   C. Changing all >= to <
   D. Interchanging all of the THEN set of instructions with the corresponding ELSE set of instructions

4. A programmer writes the instruction SUM = SUM + A(R) into a program flowchart, with R = the number of a specific element in an array, and A(R) = the Rth element of the array. The purpose of this instruction is to   4.____

   A. multiply the data items in an array by the number of elements
   B. incrementalize the elements in an array
   C. accumulate the data items in an array
   D. accumulate the elements in an array

5. The term for altering the normal sequential execution of program statements is   5.____

   A. branching   B. trailing   C. interrupting   D. indicating

6. By using the _____ logic structure, a programmer can enable a user to enter the value of a variable from the keyboard, or from a file, to select one of several options in a list.   6.____

   A. loop   B. sequential   C. case   D. decision

7. Which of the following is BASIC code used to define and reserve areas within memory to be used as program tables?   7.____

   A. RETURN   B. IF   C. REM   D. DIM

8. If a programmer overlays sections of a program on top of each other, she will also have to create a(n) _____ to access any of the modules when requested.   8.____

   A. control module   B. driver program
   C. string editor   D. nested loop

9. A HOLD instruction will be supplied for _____ modules.   9.____

    A. control-break   B. end
    C. wrapup   D. init

10. Data is initially recorded, prior to system input, on a form called the   10.____

    A. b-tree   B. primer buffer
    C. source document   D. init module

11. The _____ module processes instructions only once during a program, and only at the   11.____
    beginning.

    A. init   B. control   C. wrapup   D. read

12. A programmer should place all data needed to update a master file into a(n) _____ file.   12.____

    A. temporary   B. transaction
    C. read   D. backup

13. Which of the following instructions is used PRIMARILY in a loop logic structure?   13.____

    A. REPEAT/UNTIL   B. END/EXIT
    C. PROCESS   D. IF/THEN

14. Program processing ends at a point called the   14.____

    A. physical end   B. control-break
    C. logical end   D. hash point

15. A company maintains a sequential-accessible database. In the record data dictionary,   15.____
    each of the following items would be created as string data EXCEPT

    A. district number   B. sales amount
    C. sales date   D. salesperson name

16. In systems programming and design, developing the _____ would occur FIRST.   16.____

    A. IPO chart   B. algorithms
    C. structure chart   D. flowcharts

17. In a program flowchart, a temporary file is usually represented as   17.____

    A. HF   B. TEMP   C. F<   D. TF

18. The instruction to accumulate a variable *A* would be written   18.____

    A. COUNTER = A + 1   B. SUM = COUNTER + A
    C. COUNTER = SUM + A   D. SUM = SUM + A

19. In order to distinguish data items or data fields as separate entities, a programmer uses a   19.____
    symbol known as a(n)

    A. hash mark   B. null character
    C. delimiter   D. cursor

20. If a program uses the loop logic structure, the programmer must create a(n) _____ to   20.____
enter data to process before the loop begins.

    A. primer read   B. clear all
    C. INIT module   D. PROCESS module

21. Each array location is known as a(n)   21.____

    A. stack   B. element
    C. string   D. linked list

22. Which of the following is BASIC code used to link a data file to a program?   22.____

    A. LINK   B. OPEN   C. LET   D. GOTO

23. IF/THEN/ELSE instructions are used in programs that use the _____ logic structure.   23.____

    A. case   B. loop   C. decision   D. array

24. A(n) _____ is used in program problem-solving to stand for a memory location at which   24.____
a data value is retained.

    A. array   B. variable   C. cell   D. element

25. Which of the following is NOT a type of indicator used in systems programming?   25.____

    A. Trip value   B. Switch
    C. Nested loop   D. Flag

KEY (CORRECT ANSWERS)

1.	B	11.	A
2.	B	12.	B
3.	B	13.	A
4.	D	14.	C
5.	A	15.	B
6.	C	16.	C
7.	D	17.	A
8.	B	18.	D
9.	A	19.	C
10.	C	20.	A

21. B
22. B
23. C
24. B
25. C

EXAMINATION SECTION
TEST 1

DIRECTIONS: Each question or incomplete statement is followed by several suggested answers or completions. Select the one that BEST answers the question or completes the statement. *PRINT THE LETTER OF THE CORRECT ANSWER IN THE SPACE AT THE RIGHT.*

1. Which of the following words in a pseudocode statement can be replaced by the word *read?*

    A. Get   B. Print   C. Set   D. Store

1._____

2. Units of input and output in pseudocode are known as

    A. lines   B. items   C. strings   D. records

2._____

3. The statement required to print the value of number of students followed by the label PEOPLE would be written:

    A. Set value to *PEOPLE*
    B. Print *number of students* and *PEOPLE*
    C. Read number of students and *PEOPLE*
    D. Write number of students and *PEOPLE*

3._____

4. What command word is used to save contents of another storage location or a constant in a storage location?

    A. Store   B. Set   C. Get   D. Put

4._____

5. The symbol used for multiplication in pseudocode is

    A.   B. /   C. *   D. x

5._____

6. A statement constructed to give the first number in a data set the same value as the second number would be expressed as _____ first number _____ second number.

    A. read; as   B. set; to
    C. declare; as   D. —; =

6._____

7. The function of a literal is to

    A. read stored values
    B. identify or describe output
    C. write results
    D. store input values

7._____

8. What is the term for a grouping of items that have a similar characteristic or common identifying property?

    A. Set   B. Array
    C. String   D. Assortment

8._____

9. When calculations are written in algebraic expression, the name of the storage location in which the result would be *save* is expressed as

    A. zero   B. =   C. x   D. y

9._____

10. If a value of 10 is stored in memory at X, the output that the statement *Print 'X'* would produce is   10.____

     A. 10   B. 'X'   C. X   D. X = 10

11. Which of the following steps in using a subprogram would occur FIRST?   11.____

     A. Subprogram executed
     B. Subprogram invoked
     C. Program continues execution
     D. Results passed through program

12. A declaration for the data item *inventory item stock number* would be written: Declare   12.____

     A. stock number, numeric inventory item
     B. numeric inventory item stock number
     C. inventory item stock number
     D. character inventory item stock number

13. Of the following, a(n) _____ is NOT always an element of the *loop while* construct.   13.____

     A. *end loop* statement
     B. counter
     C. group of one or more statements forming the loop body
     D. means of making the *loop while* condition false

14. Information is placed into a storage location by means of a(n) _____ statement.   14.____

     A. call   B. assignment
     C. return   D. address

15. A programmer wants to place a zero into a memory location that is to contain a counter. Each of the following is a possible statement EXCEPT: 15.____

     A. Set counter to zero
     B. Initialize zero in counter
     C. Set COUNT to zero
     D. Store zero in counter

16. What is the term used for the items of information necessary for a program or subprogram to perform its task?   16.____

     A. Records   B. Functions
     C. Parameters   D. Constructs

17. Which of the following items of input would be needed in order to construct a module that finds the sum of two arrays, A and B? The   17.____

     A. number of elements in A and B
     B. loop for J = 1 to the number of elements in A and B
     C. two numbers, J and K
     D. sum of the two arrays

18. A statement constructed to initialize a total cost at zero would be written: 18.____

    A. Set total cost to zero   B. Set zero to total cost
    C. Total cost =0   D. Read total cost as zero

19. In order to provide a means of executing a named block of statements, the _____ is   19.____
used.

    A. call statement   B. selection parameter
    C. return statement   D. do module

20. Each element in an array is identified by a number called a _____ , which designates   20.____
position in the array.

    A. marker   B. literal
    C. string   D. subscript

21. A value of 8 is stored in memory at X.   21.____
The following statement would produce the output X = 8.

    A. Print X = 8   B. Read X as 8
    C. Print 'X =' and X   D. Print 'X = 8'

22. The symbol for division in pseudocode is   22.____

    A. —   B. ∫   C. ÷   D. /

23. A data item is denoted as non-numeric by means of a(n)   23.____

    A. record   B. string   C. address   D. name

24. A statement constructed to set the value of an employee count to zero would be written: 24.____

    A. Get zero employee count
    B. Read zero for employee count
    C. Set employee count to zero
    D. Put employee count at zero

25. Which of the following key words is NOT used for the purpose of selection in   25.____
pseudocode?

    A. Else   B. Then   C. While   D. If

KEY (CORRECT ANSWERS)

1.	A	11.	B
2.	D	12.	D
3.	D	13.	B
4.	B	14.	B
5.	C	15.	B
6.	B	16.	C
7.	B	17.	A
8.	B	18.	A
9.	C	19.	D
10.	C	20.	D

21.	C
22.	D
23.	B
24.	C
25.	C

TEST 2

DIRECTIONS: Each question or incomplete statement is followed by several suggested answers or completions. Select the one that BEST answers the question or completes the statement. *PRINT THE LETTER OF THE CORRECT ANSWER IN THE SPACE AT THE RIGHT.*

1. To perform loop operation, each of the following must be done to the counter EXCEPT   1.____

    A. division   B. initialization
    C. testing   D. incrementation

2. A subprogram that finds the largest element in an array can be constructed as a   2.____

    A. loop   B. function
    C. loop with counter   D. do module

3. *Read employee's name, hourly pay rate, number of hours worked, and gross pay.*   3.____
In the above statement, the optional word is

    A. rate   B. and   C. number   D. read

4. *Find degrees Fahrenheit by multiplying degrees centigrade by nine-fifths and adding 32*   4.____
to the result.
To compute and save the result for the above, the required statement using algebraic form would be written:

    A. F = ((9*C)/5) + 32
    B. F = (9/5)xC) + 32
    C. Set F to ((9.C/5) + 32
    D. F = 9/5C + 32

5. Output in pseudocode is indicated by each of the following key words EXCEPT   5.____

    A. print   B. get   C. write   D. put

6. The _____ statement is placed at the bottom of a selection group.   6.____

    A. call   B. return   C. do   D. end if

7. A statement constructed to save 100 in number of people would be written: 7.____

    A. Read 100 for number of people
    B. Store 100 for number of people
    C. Set 100 for number of people
    D. Set number of people to 100

8. In pseudocode, the *loop with counter* construct is specified by the key words   8.____

    A. loop while   B. end loop
    C. loop for   D. end if

9. A programmer wishes to construct a nested selection to handle the following case: Add 1   9.____
to senior resident counter when town residence is Oakville and person's age is greater than 64.
In the best logical construction, the statement would begin:

A. Others counter = others counter + 1
B. If town of residence is Oakville
C. If age is greater than 64
D. Senior residence counter = senior resident counter + 1

10. Which of the following terms is NOT used to indicate the meaning of output in pseudocode?   10._____

A. Character string   B. Label
C. Record   D. Literal

11. What kind of statement is used to revert control to a calling program?   11._____

A. Call   B. End loop
C. Return   D. Reassignment

12. The statement required to save the literal SUSPENDED in student status would be written: 12._____

A. Write student status as SUSPENDED
B. Get SUSPENDED to student status
C. Set student status to 'SUSPENDED'
D. Read student status as 'SUSPENDED'

13. Which of the following words in a pseudocode statement can be replaced by the word *print*?   13._____

A. Get   B. Print   C. Set   D. Store

14. In pseudocode, the = symbol indicates   14._____

A. division
B. an equality of values
C. a read command
D. a storage assignment for information

15. Which of the following steps in using a subprogram would occur LAST?   15._____

A. Subprogram executed
B. Subprogram invoked
C. Program continues execution
D. Results passed through program

16. If a value of 10 is stored in memory at X, the statement *Print X* will produce the output   16._____

A. 10   B. 'X'   C. X   D. X = 10

17. Which of the following is NOT an example of a non-numeric data item?   17._____

A. Telephone number
B. ZIP code
C. Student identification number
D. Temperature

18. For moving the contents of one storage location to another location in algebraic expression, a statement of the form _____ should be used.   18.____

    A. x = y   B. Move x to y
    C. x/y   D. Set x to y

19. A declaration for the data item *number of employees* would be written: Declare   19.____

    A. employees, number of
    B. numeric number of employees
    C. number of employees
    D. character number of employees

20. In a *loop while* construct, the loop will be terminated upon the introduction of a(n)   20.____

    A. false condition   B. return statement
    C. subprogram   D. *end if* statement

21. The statement required to print the message GROSS PAY IS $ followed by the value of gross pay would be written: 21.____

    A. Get gross pay and GROSS PAY IS $
    B. Read 'GROSS PAY IS $' and gross pay
    C. Write 'GROSS PAY IS $' and gross pay
    D. Print 'GROSS PAY IS $' and gross pay

22. In pseudocode, the value x^2 would be written   22.____

    A. X-2   B. X**2   C. X//2   D. X*2

23. A statement using algebraic form to compute and save the result for *Add one to number of days* would be written: 23.____

    A. Number of days + 1
    B. Number of days = number of days + 1
    C. Set number of days to number of days + 1
    D. Set number of days + 1

24. What type of statement is used to invoke a subprogram?   24.____

    A. Do   B. Call
    C. Assignment   D. Return

25. A programmer wants to construct a statement that instructs the computer to print the message *There is no sales tax* if the tax code is zero and *The sales tax is 4%* otherwise. In the statement, what would follow the key word *else?*   25.____

    A. Write 'There is no sales tax'
    B. Get tax code
    C. Write 'The sales tax is 4%'
    D. Set tax code to zero

KEY (CORRECT ANSWERS)

1.	A	11.	C
2.	B	12.	C
3.	B	13.	B
4.	A	14.	D
5.	B	15.	C
6.	D	16.	A
7.	D	17.	D
8.	C	18.	A
9.	C	19.	B
10.	C	20.	A

21.	C
22.	B
23.	B
24.	B
25.	C

READING COMPREHENSION
UNDERSTANDING AND INTERPRETING WRITTEN MATERIAL
EXAMINATION SECTION
TEST 1

DIRECTIONS: Each question or incomplete statement is followed by several suggested answers or completions. Select the one that BEST answers the question or completes the statement. *PRINT THE LETTER OF THE CORRECT ANSWER IN THE SPACE AT THE RIGHT.*

Questions 1-7.

DIRECTIONS: Questions 1 through 7 are to be answered SOLELY on the basis of the following passage.

The first step in establishing a programming development schedule is to rate the programs to be developed or to be maintained on the basis of complexity, size, and input-output complexity. The most experienced programmer should rate the program complexity based on the system flow chart. The same person should do all of the rating so that all programs are rated in the same manner. If possible, the same person who rates the complexity should estimate the program size based on the number of pages of coding. This rating can easily be checked, after coding has been completed, against the number of pages of coding actually produced. If there is consistent error in the estimates for program size, all future estimates should be corrected for this error or the estimating method reviewed.

The input-output rating is a mechanical count of the number of input and output units or tapes which the program uses. The objective is to measure the number of distinct files which the program must control.

After the ratings have been completed, the man-days required for each of the tasks can be calculated. Good judgment or, if available, a table of past experience is used to translate the ratings into man-days, the units in which the schedule is expressed. The calculations should keep the values for each task completely separate so that a later evaluation can be made by program, programmer, and function.

After the values have been calculated, it is a simple matter to establish a development schedule. This can be a simple bar chart which assigns work to specific programmers, a complex computer program using the *PERT* technique of critical path scheduling, or other useful type of document.

1.   The rating and estimating of the programs should be performed by   1.____

    A.   the person who will do the programming
    B.   a programmer trainee
    C.   the most experienced programmer
    D.   the operations supervisor

2. The measurement used to express the programming schedule is the number of   2.____

    A. distinct files controlled by the programmer
    B. man-days
    C. pages of coding
    D. programmers

3. A mechanical count of the number of input and output units or tapes should be consid-   3.____
ered as a(n)

    A. input-output rating
    B. measure of the number of man-days required
    C. rating of complexity
    D. estimate of the number of pages of coding

4. Programming development scheduling methods are for   4.____

    A. new programs only
    B. programs to be developed and maintained
    C. large and complicated programs only
    D. maintenance programs only

5. If there is a consistent error in the estimates for program size, all estimates should be   5.____

    A. adjusted for future programs
    B. eliminated for all programs
    C. replaced by rating of complexity
    D. replaced by input-output rating

6. It is intimated that   6.____

    A. the calculations should keep the valuations for each task completely separated
    B. it is a simple matter to establish a development schedule
    C. the man-days required for each of the tasks can be calculated
    D. a later evaluation will be made

7. Complexity of programs can be checked   7.____

    A. before coding has been completed
    B. after future estimates have been corrected for error
    C. as a first step in establishing a complex computer program
    D. with reference to the number of pages of coding produced

Questions 8-13.

DIRECTIONS: Questions 8 through 13 are to be answered SOLELY on the basis of the follow-
                 ing passage.

    The purposes of program testing are to determine that the program has been coded cor-
rectly, that the coding matches the logical design, and that the logical design matches the
basic requirements of the job as set down in the specifications. Program errors fall into the following categories: errors in logic, clerical errors, misidentification of the computer components' functions, misinterpretation of the requirements of the job, and system analysis errors.

The number of errors in a program will average one for each 125 instructions, assuming that the programmer has been reasonably careful in his coding system. The number of permutations and combinations of conditions in a program may reach into the billions before each possibility has been thoroughly checked out. It is, therefore, a practical impossibility to check out each and every possible combination of conditions—the effort would take years, even in the simplest program. As a result, it is quite possible for errors to remain latent for a number of years, suddenly appearing when a particular combination is reached which had not previously occurred.

Latent program errors will remain in operating programs, and their occurrence should be minimized by complete and thorough testing. The fact that the program is operative and reaches end-of-job satisfactorily does not mean that all of the exception conditions and their permutations and combinations have been tested. Quite the contrary, many programs reach end-of-job after very few tests, since the *straight-line* part of the program is often simplest. However, the exceptions programmed to deal with a minimal percentage of the input account for a large percentage of the instructions. It is, therefore, quite possible to reach the end-of-job halt with only 10% of the program checked out.

8. One of the MAIN points of this passage is that   8._____

    A. it is impossible to do a good job of programming
    B. reaching end-of-job means only 10% of the program is checked out
    C. standard testing procedures should require testing of every possible combination of conditions
    D. elimination of all errors can never be assured, but the occurrence of errors can be minimized by thorough testing

9. Latent program errors GENERALLY   9._____

    A. evade detection for some time
    B. are detected in the last test run
    C. test the number of permutations and combinations in a program
    D. allow the program to go to end-of-job

10. Which one of the following statements pertaining to errors in a program is CORRECT?   10._____

    A. If the program has run to a normal completion, then all program errors have been eliminated.
    B. Program errors, if not caught in testing, will surely be detected in the first hundred runs of the program.
    C. It is practically impossible to verify that the typical program is free of errors.
    D. A program that is coded correctly is free of errors.

11. Among other things, program testing is designed to   11._____

    A. assure that the documentation is correct
    B. assure that the coding is correct
    C. determine the program running time
    D. measure programmer's performance

12. The difficulty in detecting errors in programs is due to

    12.____

    A. the extremely large number of conditions that exist in a program
    B. poor analysis of work errors
    C. very sophisticated and clever programming
    D. reaching the end-of-job halt with only 10% of the program checked out

13. If the program being tested finally reaches the end-of-job halt, it means that

    13.____

    A. one path through the program has been successfully tested
    B. less than 10% of the program has been tested
    C. the program has been coded correctly
    D. the logical design is correct

Questions 14-20.

DIRECTIONS: Questions 14 through 20 are to be answered SOLELY on the basis of the following passage.

Systems analysis represents a major link in the chain of translations from the problem to its machine solution. After the problem and its requirements for solution have been stated in clear terms, the systems analyst defines the broad outlines of the machine solution. He must know the overall capabilities of the equipment, and he must be familiar with the application. The ultimate output of the analysis is a detailed job specification containing all the tools necessary to produce a series of computer programs. The purpose of the specifications is to document and describe the system by defining the problem and the proposed solution, explain system outputs and functions, state system requirements for programmers, and to avoid misunderstandings among involved departments. The specification serves as a link between the analysis of the problem and the next function, programming. Systems analysis relies on creativity rather than rote analysis to develop effective computer systems. But this creativity must be channeled and documented effectively if lasting value is to be obtained.

14. According to the above paragraph, the systems analyst MUST be familiar with

    14.____

    A. programming and the machine solution
    B. the machine solution and the next function
    C. the application and programming
    D. the application and the equipment capabilities

15. According to the above paragraph, the time that systems analysis MUST be performed is

    15.____

    A. *after* the problem analysis
    B. *after* programming
    C. *before* problem definition
    D. *before* problem analysis

16. According to the above paragraph, the MAIN task performed by the systems analyst is to

    16.____

    A. write the program
    B. analyze the problem
    C. define the overall capacities of the equipment
    D. define the machine solution of the problem

17. According to the above paragraph, the document produced by the systems analyst as his main output does NOT normally include   17.____

    A. an explanation of system outputs
    B. system requirements for programmers
    C. a statement of the problem
    D. performance standards

18. According to the above paragraph, the systems analysis function is   18.____

    A. relatively straightforward, requiring little creative effort
    B. extremely complex, making standard procedures impossible
    C. primarily a rote memory procedure
    D. a creative effort

19. According to the above paragraph, the specification   19.____

    A. is a major link in the sequence from problem to machine solution
    B. states the problem and its requirements for solution
    C. is chiefly concerned with the overall capabilities of the equipment
    D. represents the ultimate product of systems analysis

20. According to the above paragraph, the sequential function after the analysis of the program is   20.____

    A. documentation   B. application
    C. definition   D. programming

Questions 21-25.

DIRECTIONS: Questions 21 through 25 are to be answered SOLELY on the basis of the following passage.

Currently, memory represents one of the main limitations on computer performance and, as a result, is one of the areas where technological improvements will prove most fruitful.

Historically, the main problem of computer memories has been a very unfavorable cost-to-speed ratio. Memory devices which have great speed cost disproportionately more than those with less speed. This problem has forced computer designers to use minimum amounts of rapid access memory and to rely mainly on slower, large capacity storage. This practice has resulted in a *memory tree,* where a hierarchy of memory devices provides various increments of storage at different costs and speeds for various purposes.

To achieve better speed/cost ratios, designers are increasingly turning to memory media other than the traditional ferrite cores. These cores now account for over 90% of the memory market. Plated wire and semiconductors are the media most likely to supplant ferrite cores. Semiconductors are expected to rapidly displace cores, starting with higher speed memories. Their costs are dropping sharply and are expected to drop as much as five-fold by the middle of this decade, while their speeds are at least doubling.

Despite the increasing use of competing technologies, ferrite cores will probably still dominate the extended random access storage area. Since the largest increment of storage is associated with ferrite core memory devices, their share of the internal memory market was well over 50% by 1980. The only factor militating against this is the possibility that the largest manufacturers of computers may abandon the extended internal storage concept.

Memory developments likely to happen later in this decade include the progressive replacement of magnetic drums by magnetic disks. The latter were themselves displaced near the end of the seventies by electro optical units, followed by magnetic bubble storage. It also may prove possible to show the feasibility of associative processors. Under this concept, which is still experimental, data access would be considerably speeded through use of Contents-Addressable-Memories (CAM).

21. According to the above passage, a hierarchy of memory devices which provides various increments of storage at different costs and speeds has been used by designers because

    A. one of the larger manufacturers of computers might abandon the extended internal storage concept
    B. of the very unfavorable cost-to-speed ratio of computer memories
    C. magnetic disks have progressively replaced magnetic drums in the mid-seventies
    D. data access is expected to be appreciably speeded up through the use of Content-Addressable-Memories

21._____

22. According to the above passage, which of the following memory developments is MOST likely to have occurred by 1980?

    A. Designers will turn to memories other than core for 90% of their needs.
    B. Cores and semiconductors will largely replace plated wire memories.
    C. Cores and semiconductors will largely be replaced by electro optical and magnetic bubble storage.
    D. Ferrite core will continue to dominate the internal memory market.

22._____

23. According to the above passage, the speed/cost ratio for semiconductors is

    A. becoming more favorable
    B. the same as the speed/cost ratio for plated wire
    C. remaining constant
    D. less favorable than the speed/cost ratio for ferrite core

23._____

24. According to the information in the passage, development of improved memory technology is IMPORTANT because

    A. it demonstrates the feasibility of associative processors
    B. memory represents one of the chief limitations on computer performance today
    C. semiconductors are expected to largely replace core which now represents about half of the memory market
    D. data can now be speeded through the use of CAM

24._____

25. Three types of memory media which are discussed in the above passage are

    A. core, plated wire, semiconductors
    B. high speed buffer, magnetic disks, rotating magnetic storage
    C. ferrite cores, magnetic drums, remote data terminals
    D. high speed buffers, magnetic disks, magnetic drums

25._____

_____

KEY (CORRECT ANSWERS)

1.	C		11.	B
2.	B		12.	A
3.	A		13.	A
4.	B		14.	D
5.	A		15.	A
6.	D		16.	D
7.	D		17.	D
8.	D		18.	D
9.	A		19.	D
10.	C		20.	D

21.	B
22.	D
23.	A
24.	B
25.	A

———

TEST 2

Questions 1-5.

DIRECTIONS: Questions 1 through 5 are to be answered SOLELY on the basis of the following paragraph.

Work standards presuppose an ability to measure work. Measurement in office management is needed for several reasons. First, it is necessary to evaluate the overall efficiency of the office itself. It is then essential to measure the efficiency of each particular section or unit and that of the individual worker. To plan and control the work of sections and units, one must have measurement. A program of measurement goes hand in hand with a program of standards. One can have measurement without standards, but one cannot have work standards without measurement. Providing data on amount of work done and time expended, measurement does not deal with the amount of energy expended by an individual although, in many cases, such energy may be in direct proportion to work output. Usually from two-thirds to three-fourths of all work can be measured. However, less than two-thirds of all work is actually measured because measurement difficulties are encountered when office work is non-repetitive and irregular, or when it is primarily mental rather than manual. These obstacles are often used as excuses for non-measurement far more frequently than is justified.

1. According to the above paragraph, an office manager cannot set work standards unless he can   1._____

    A. plan the amount of work to be done
    B. control the amount of work that is done
    C. estimate accurately the quantity of work done
    D. delegate the amount of work to be done to efficient workers

2. According to the above paragraph, the type of office work that would be MOST difficult to measure would be   2._____

    A. checking warrants for accuracy of information
    B. recording payroll changes
    C. processing applications
    D. making up a new system of giving out supplies

3. According to the above paragraph, the ACTUAL amount of work that is measured is _____ of all work.   3._____

    A. less than two-thirds
    B. two-thirds to three-fourths
    C. less than three-sixths
    D. more than three-fourths

4. Which of the following would be MOST difficult to determine by using measurement techniques?   4._____

    A. The amount of work that is accomplished during a certain period of time
    B. The amount of work that should be planned for a period of time
    C. How much time is needed to do a certain task
    D. The amount of incentive a person must have to do his job

5. The one of the following which is the MOST suitable title for the above paragraph is   5.____

    A. HOW MEASUREMENT OF OFFICE EFFICIENCY DEPENDS ON WORK STAN-
        DARDS
    B. USING MEASUREMENT FOR OFFICE MANAGEMENT AND EFFICIENCY
    C. WORK STANDARDS AND THE EFFICIENCY OF THE OFFICE WORKER
    D. MANAGING THE OFFICE USING MEASURED WORK STANDARDS

Questions 6-9.

DIRECTIONS: Questions 6 through 9 are to be answered SOLELY on the basis of the follow-
                ing passage.

    Work measurement concerns accomplishment or productivity. It has to do with results; it does not deal with the amount of energy used up, although in many cases this may be in direct proportion to the work output. Work measurement not only helps a manager to distribute work loads fairly, but it also enables him to define work success in actual units, evaluate employee performance, and determine where corrective help is needed. Work measurement is accomplished by measuring the amount produced, measuring the time spent to produce it, and relating the two. To illustrate, it is common to speak of so many orders processed within a given time. The number of orders processed becomes meaningful when related to the amount of time taken.

    Much of the work in an office can be measured fairly accurately and inexpensively. The extent of work measurement possible in any given case will depend upon the particular type of office tasks performed, but usually from two-thirds to three-fourths of all work in an office can be measured. It is true that difficulty in work measurement is encountered, for example, when the office work is irregular and not repeated often, or when the work is primarily mental rather than manual. These are problems, but they are used as excuses for doing no work measurement far more frequently than is justified.

6. According to the above passage, which of the following BEST illustrates the type of information obtained as a result of work measurement?   6.____

    A. Clerk takes one hour to file 150 folders
    B. Typist types five letters
    C. Stenographer works harder typing from shorthand notes than she does typing from
        a typed draft
    D. Clerk keeps track of employees' time by computing sick leave, annual leave, and
        overtime leave

7. The above passage does NOT indicate that work measurement can be used to help a   7.____
   supervisor to determine

    A. *why* an employee is performing poorly on the job
    B. *who* are the fast and slow workers in the unit
    C. *how* the work in the unit should be divided up
    D. *how* long it should take to perform a certain task

8. According to the above passage, the kind of work that would be MOST difficult to mea-   8.____
   sure would be such work as

A. sorting mail
B. designing a form for a new procedure
C. photocopying various materials
D. answering inquiries with form letters

9. The excuses mentioned in the above passage for failure to perform work measurement can be BEST summarized as the   9._____

A. repetitive nature of office work
B. costs involved in carrying out accurate work measurement
C. inability to properly use the results obtained from work measurement
D. difficulty involved in measuring certain types of work

Questions 10-13.

DIRECTIONS: Questions 10 through 13 are to be answered SOLELY on the basis of the following passage.

Job analysis combined with performance appraisal is an excellent method of determining training needs of individuals. The steps in this method are to determine the specific duties of the job, to evaluate the adequacy with which the employee performs each of these duties, and finally to determine what significant improvements can be made by training.

The list of duties can be obtained in a number of ways: asking the employee, asking the supervisor, observing the employee, etc. Adequacy of performance can be estimated by the employee, but the supervisor's evaluation must also be obtained. This evaluation will usually be based on observation.

What does the supervisor observe? The employee, while he is working; the employee's work relationships; the ease, speed, and sureness of the employee's actions; the way he applies himself to the job; the accuracy and amount of completed work, its conformity with established procedures and standards; the appearance of the work; the soundness of judgment it shows; and, finally, signs of good or poor communication, understanding, and cooperation among employees.

Such observation is a normal and inseparable part of the everyday job of supervision. Systematically recorded, evaluated, and summarized, it highlights both general and individual training needs.

10. According to the above passage, job analysis may be used by the supervisor in   10._____

A. increasing his own understanding of tasks performed in his unit
B. increasing efficiency of communication within the organization
C. assisting personnel experts in the classification of positions
D. determining in which areas an employee needs more instruction

11. According to the above passage, the FIRST step in determining the training needs of employees is to   11._____

A. locate the significant improvements that can be made by training
B. determine the specific duties required in a job
C. evaluate the employee's performance
D. motivate the employee to want to improve himself

12. On the basis of the above passage, which of the following is the BEST way for a supervisor to determine the adequacy of employee performance?   12._____

    A. Check the accuracy and amount of completed work
    B. Ask the training officer
    C. Observe all aspects of the employee's work
    D. Obtain the employee's own estimate

13. Which of the following is NOT mentioned by the above passage as a factor to be taken into consideration in judging the adequacy of employee performance?   13._____

    A. Accuracy of completed work
    B. Appearance of completed work
    C. Cooperation among employees
    D. Attitude of the employee toward his supervisor

Questions 14-15.

DIRECTIONS: Questions 14 and 15 are to be answered SOLELY on the basis of the following paragraph.

    The fundamental characteristic of the type of remote control which management needs to bridge the gap between itself and actual operations is the more effective use of records and reports – more specifically, the gathering and interpretation of the facts contained in records and reports. Facts, for management purposes, are those data (narrative and quantitative) which express in simple terms the current standing of the agency's program, work, and resources in relation to the plans and policies formulated by management. They are those facts or measures (1) which permit management to compare current status with past performance and with its forecasts for the immediate future, and (2) which provide management with a reliable basis for long-range forecasting.

14. For management purposes, facts are, according to the above paragraph,   14._____

    A. forecasts which can be compared to current status
    B. data which can be used for certain control purposes
    C. a fundamental characteristic of a type of remote control
    D. the data contained in records and reports

15. An inference which can be drawn from this statement is that   15._____

    A. management which has a reliable basis for long-range forecasting has at its disposal a type of remote control which is needed to bridge the gap between itself and actual operations
    B. data which do not express in simple terms the current standing of the agency's program, work, and resources in relationship to the plans and policies formulated by management may still be facts for management purposes
    C. data which express relationships among the agency's program, work, and resources are management facts
    D. the gap between management and actual operations can only be bridged by characteristics which are fundamentally a type of remote control

Questions 16-17.

DIRECTIONS: Questions 16 and 17 are to be answered SOLELY on the basis of the following
                      passage.

Two approaches are available in developing criteria for the evaluation of plans. One
approach, designated Approach A, is a review and analysis of characteristics that differenti-
ate successful plans from unsuccessful plans. These criteria are descriptive in nature and
serve as a checklist against which the plan under consideration may be judged. These characteristics have been observed by many different students of planning, and there is considerable agreement concerning the characteristics necessary for a plan to be successful.

A second approach to the development of criteria for judging plans, designated
Approach B, is the determination of the degree to which the plan under consideration is economic. The word *economic* is used here in its broadest sense; i.e., effective in its utilization of
resources. In order to determine the economic worth of a plan, it is necessary to use a technique that permits the description of any plan in economic terms and to utilize this technique
to the extent that it becomes a *way of thinking* about plans.

16. According to Approach B, the MOST successful plan is *generally* one which   16._____

         A. costs least to implement
         B. gives most value for resources expended
         C. uses the least expensive resources
         D. utilizes the greatest number of resources

17. According to Approach A, a successful plan is one which is   17._____

         A. descriptive in nature
         B. lowest in cost
         C. similar to other successful plans
         D. agreed upon by many students of planning

Questions 18-20.

DIRECTIONS: Questions 18 through 20 are to be answered SOLELY on the basis of the fol-
                      lowing passage.

The primary purpose of control reports is to supply information intended to serve as the
basis for corrective action if needed. At the same time, the significance of control reports
must be kept in proper perspective. Control reports are only a part of the planning-manage-
ment information system. Control information includes nonfinancial as well as financial data
that measure performance and isolate variances from standard. Control information also provides feedback so that planning information may be updated and corrected. Whenever possible, control reports should be designed so that they provide feedback for the planning
process as well as provide information of immediate value to the control process.

Since the culmination of the control process is the taking of necessary corrective action
to bring performance in line with standards, it follows that control information must be directed
to the person who is organizationally responsible for taking the required action. Usually the
same information, though in a somewhat abbreviated form, is given to the responsible man-

ager's superior. A district sales manager needs a complete daily record of the performance of each of his salesmen; yet, the report forwarded to the regional sales manager summarizes only the performance of each sales district in his region. In preparing reports for higher echelons of management, summary statements and recommendations for action should appear on the first page; substantiating data, usually the information presented to the person directly responsible for the operation, may be included if needed.

18. A control report serves its primary purpose as part of the process which leads DIRECTLY to

    18.____

    A. better planning for future action
    B. increasing the performance of district salesmen
    C. the establishment of proper performance standards
    D. taking corrective action when performance is poor

19. The one of the following which would be the BEST description of a control report is that a control report is a form of

    19.____

    A. planning
    C. direction
    B. communication
    D. organization

20. If control reports are to be effective, the one of the following which is LEAST essential to the effectiveness of control reporting is a system of

    20.____

    A. communication
    C. authority
    B. standards
    D. work simplification

Questions 21-23.

DIRECTIONS: Questions 21 through 23 are to be answered SOLELY on the basis of the following passage.

The need for the best in management techniques has given rise to the expression *scientific management*. Within reasonable limits, management can be scientific, but it will probably be many decades before it becomes truly scientific either in the factory or in the office. As long as it is impossible to measure accurately individual performance and to equate human behavior, so long will it be impossible to develop completely scientific techniques of office management. There is a likelihood, of course, that management might be reduced to a science when it is applied to inanimate objects which facilitate operations such as machinery, office equipment and furnishings, and forms. The limiting factor, therefore, is the human element.

21. The above passage is concerned PRIMARILY with the

    21.____

    A. value of scientific office management
    B. methods for the development of scientific office management
    C. need for the best office management techniques
    D. possibility of reducing office management to a science

22. According to the above passage, the realization of truly scientific office management is dependent upon the

    22.____

    A. expression of management techniques
    B. development of accurate personnel measurement techniques

C. passage of many decades, most probably
D. elimination of individual differences in human behavior

23. According to the above passage, the scientific management of inanimate objects   23._____

    A. occurs automatically because there is no human factor
    B. cannot occur in a factory, but can occur in an office
    C. could be achieved without the concurrent achievement of truly scientific office management
    D. is not a necessary component of truly scientific office management

Questions 24-25.

DIRECTIONS: Questions 24 and 25 are to be answered SOLELY on the basis of the following paragraph.

     Your role as human resources utilization experts is to submit your techniques to operating administrators, for the program must, in reality, be theirs, not yours. We, in personnel, have been guilty of encouraging operating executives to believe that these important matters affecting their employees are personnel department matters, not management matters. We should hardly be surprised, as a consequence, to find these executives playing down the role of personnel and finding personnel routines a nuisance, for these are not in the mainstream of managing the enterprise – or so we have encouraged them to believe.

24. The BEST of the following interpretations of the above paragraph is that   24._____

    A. personnel people have been guilty of *passing the buck* on personnel functions
    B. operating officials have difficulty understanding personnel techniques
    C. personnel employees have tended to usurp some functions rightfully belonging to management
    D. matters affecting employees should be handled by the personnel department

25. The BEST of the following interpretations of the above paragraph is that   25._____

    A. personnel departments have aided and abetted the formulation of negative attitudes on the part of management
    B. personnel people are labor relations experts and should carry out these duties
    C. personnel activities are not really the responsibility of management
    D. management is now being encouraged by personnel experts to assume some responsibility for personnel functions

KEY (CORRECT ANSWERS)

1.	C		11.	B
2.	D		12.	C
3.	A		13.	D
4.	D		14.	B
5.	B		15.	C
6.	A		16.	B
7.	A		17.	C
8.	B		18.	D
9.	D		19.	B
10.	D		20.	D

21.	D
22.	B
23.	C
24.	C
25.	A

TEST 3

DIRECTIONS: Each question or incomplete statement is followed by several suggested answers or completions. Select the one that BEST answers the question or completes the statement. *PRINT THE LETTER OF THE CORRECT ANSWER IN THE SPACE AT THE RIGHT.*

Questions 1-3

DIRECTIONS: Questions 1 through 3 are to be answered SOLELY on the basis of the following paragraph.

Prior to revising its child care program, a department feels that it is necessary to get some information from the mothers served by the existing program in order to determine where changes are required. A questionnaire is to be constructed to obtain this information.

1. Of the following points which can be taken into consideration in the construction of the questionnaire, the one which is of LEAST importance is

    A. that the data are to be put into punch cards
    B. the aspects of the program which seem to be in need of change
    C. the type of person who will fill out the questionnaire
    D. testing the questionnaire for ambiguity in advance of general distribution
    E. setting up a control group so that answers received can be compared to a standard

1.____

2. To discuss this questionnaire with all mothers who have been asked to answer it, before they actually fill it out, is

    A. *desirable;* the mothers may be able to offer valuable suggestions for changes in the form of the questionnaire
    B. *undesirable;* it is of some value but consumes too much valuable time
    C. *desirable;* cooperation and uniform interpretation will tend to be achieved
    D. *undesirable;* it may cause the answers to be biased
    E. *desirable;* the group will tend to support the program

2.____

3. Of the following items included in the questionnaire, the one which will be of LEAST assistance for comparing attitudes toward the program among different kinds of persons is

    A. name   B. address   C. age
    D. place of birth   E. education

3.____

Questions 4-6.

DIRECTIONS: Questions 4 through 6 are to be answered SOLELY on the basis of the following paragraph.

The supervisor of a large clerical and statistical division has assigned to one of the units under his supervision the preparation of a special statistical report required by the department head. The unit head accepted the assignment without comment but soon ran into considerable difficulty because no one in his unit had had any statistical training.

4. If a result of this lack of training is that the report is not completed on time, although everyone has done all that could be expected, the responsibility for the failure rests with

    A. the department head   B. the supervisor
    C. the unit head   D. the employees in the unit
    E. no one

4.____

5. This incident indicates that the supervisory staff has insufficient knowledge of employee   5._____

    A. capabilities
    B. reaction to increased demands
    C. on-the-job training needs
    D. work habits
    E. ability to perform ordinary assignments

6. After working on the report for two days, the unit head notifies the supervisor that he will   6._____
not be able to get the report out in the required time. He states that his staff will be completely trained in another day or two and that after that preparing the report will be a simple matter. At this stage, the supervisor decides to have the statistical unit prepare the
report. This action on the part of the supervisor is

    A. *undesirable;* the unit head should be given an incentive to continue with his training
       program which may produce good results
    B. *desirable;* it is the most effective way in which the supervisor can show his displea-
       sure with the unit head's failure
    C. *undesirable;* it may adversely affect the morale of the unit
    D. *desirable;* it will generally result in a better report completed in a shorter time
    E. *undesirable;* the time spent on training the unit will be completely wasted

Questions 7-9.

DIRECTIONS: Questions 7 through 9 are to be answered SOLELY on the basis of the follow-
                ing paragraph.

    The regressive uses of discipline are ubiquitous. Administrative architects who seek the
optimum balance between structure and morale must accordingly look toward the identification and isolation of disciplinary elements. The whole range of disciplinary sanctions, from the
reprimand to the dismissal, presents opportunities for reciprocity and accommodation of insti-
tutional interests. When rightly seized upon, these opportunities may provide the moment and
the means for fruitful exercise of leadership and collaboration.

7. The one of the following ways of reworking the ideas presented in the above paragraph in   7._____
order to be BEST suited for presentation in an in-service training course in supervision
is:

    A. When one of your men does something wrong, talk it over with him. Tell him what
       he should have done. This is a chance for you to show the man that you are on his
       side and that you would welcome him on your side.
    B. It is not necessary to reprimand or to dismiss an employee because he needs dis-
       ciplining. The alert foreman will lead and collaborate with his subordinates, making
       discipline unnecessary.
    C. A good way to lead the men you supervise is to take those opportunities which
       present themselves to use the whole range of disciplinary sanctions from repri-
       mand to dismissal as a means for enforcing collaboration.
    D. Chances to punish a man in your squad should be welcomed as opportunities to
       show that you are a *good guy* who does not bear a grudge.
    E. Before you talk to a man or have him report to the office for something he has done
       wrong, attempt to lead him and get him to work with you. Tell him that his actions
       were wrong, that you expect him not to repeat the same wrong act, and that you
       will take a firmer stand if the act is repeated.

8. Of the following, the PRINCIPAL point made in the paragraph above is that   8._____

   A. discipline is frequently used improperly
   B. it is possible to isolate the factors entering into a disciplinary situation
   C. identification of the disciplinary elements is desirable
   D. disciplinary situations may be used to the advantage of the organization
   E. obtaining the best relationship between organizational form and spirit depends upon the ability to label disciplinary elements

9. The MOST novel idea presented in the above paragraph is that   9._____

   A. discipline is rarely necessary
   B. discipline may be a joint action of man and supervisor
   C. there are disciplinary elements which may be identified
   D. a range of disciplinary sanctions exists
   E. it is desirable to seek for balance between structure and morale.

Questions 10-11.

DIRECTIONS: Questions 10 and 11 are to be answered SOLELY on the basis of the following paragraph.

   People must be selected to do the tasks involved and must be placed on a payroll in jobs fairly priced. Each of these people must be assigned those tasks which he can perform best; the work of each must be appraised, and good and poor work singled out appropriately. Skill in performing assigned tasks must be developed, and the total work situation must be conducive to sustained high performance. Finally, employees must be separated from the work force either voluntarily or involuntarily because of inefficient or unsatisfactory performance or because of curtailment of organizational activities.

10. A personnel function which is NOT included in the above description is   10._____

   A. classification   B. training   C. placement
   D. severance   E. service rating

11. The underlying implied purpose of the policy enunciated in the above paragraph is   11._____

   A. to plan for the curtailment of the organizational program when it becomes necessary
   B. to single out appropriate skill in performing assigned tasks
   C. to develop and maintain a high level of performance by employees
   D. that training employees in relation to the total work situation is essential if good and poor work are to be singled out
   E. that equal money for equal work results in a total work situation which insures proper appraisal

Questions 12-16.

DIRECTIONS: Questions 12 through 16 are to be answered SOLELY on the basis of the following sections which appeared in a report on the work production of two bureaus of a department. Throughout the report, assume that each month has 4 weeks.

Each of the two bureaus maintains a chronological file. In Bureau A, every 9 months on the average, this material fills a standard legal size file cabinet sufficient for 12,000 work units. In Bureau B, the same type of cabinet is filled in 18 months. Each bureau maintains three complete years of information plus a current file. When the current file cabinet is filled, the cabinet containing the oldest material is emptied, the contents disposed of, and the cabinet used for current material. The similarity of these operations makes it possible to consolidate these files with little effort.

Study of the practice of using typists as filing clerks for periods when there is no typing work showed (1) Bureau A has for the past 6 months completed a total of 1500 filing work units a week using on the average 200 man-hours of trained file clerk time and 20 man-hours of typist time, (2) Bureau B has in the same period completed a total of 2000 filing work units a week using on the average 125 man-hours of trained file clerk time and 60 hours of typist time. This includes all work in chronological files. Assuming that all clerks work at the same speed and that all typists work at the same speed, this indicates that work other than filing should be found for typists or that they should be given some training in the filing procedures used.... It should be noted that Bureau A has not been producing the 1,600 units of technical (not filing) work per 30 day period required by Schedule K, but is at present 200 units behind. The Bureau should be allowed 3 working days to get on schedule.

12. What percentage (approximate) of the total number of filing work units completed in both units consists of the work involved in the maintenance of the chronological files?   12.____

    A. 5%   B. 10%   C. 15%   D. 20%   E. 25%

13. If the two chronological files are consolidated, the number of months which should be allowed for filling a cabinet is   13.____

    A. 2   B. 4   C. 6   D. 8   E. 14

14. The MAXIMUM number of file cabinets which can be released for other uses as a result of the consolidation recommended is   14.____

    A. 0
    B. 1
    C. 2
    D. 3
    E. not determinable on the basis of the data given

15. If all the filing work for both units is consolidated without any diminution in the amount to be done and all filing work is done by trained file clerks, the number of clerks required (35-hour work week) is   15.____

    A. 4   B. 5   C. 6   D. 7   E. 8

16. In order to comply with the recommendation with respect to Schedule K, the present work production of Bureau A must be increased by   16.____

    A. 50%   B. 100%
    C. 150%   D. 200%
    E. an amount which is not determinable on the basis of the data given

Questions 17-18.

DIRECTIONS: Questions 17 and 18 are to be answered SOLELY on the basis of the following paragraph.

Production planning is mainly a process of synthesis. As a basis for the positive act of bringing complex production elements properly together, however, analysis is necessary, especially if improvement is to be made in an existing organization. The necessary analysis requires customary means of orientation and preliminary fact gathering with emphasis, however, on the recognition of administrative goals and of the relationship among work steps.

17. The entire process described is PRIMARILY one of   17.____

    A. taking apart, examining, and recombining
    B. deciding what changes are necessary, making the changes and checking on their value
    C. fact finding so as to provide the necessary orientation
    D. discovering just where the emphasis in production should be placed and then modifying the existing procedure so that it is placed properly
    E. recognizing administrative goals and the relationship among work steps

18. In production planning, according to the above paragraph, analysis is used PRIMARILY as   18.____

    A. a means of making important changes in an organization
    B. the customary means of orientation and preliminary fact finding
    C. a development of the relationship among work steps
    D. a means for holding the entire process intact by providing a logical basis
    E. a method to obtain the facts upon which a theory can be built

Questions 19-21.

DIRECTIONS: Questions 19 through 21 are to be answered SOLELY on the basis of the following paragraph.

Public administration is policy-making. But it is not autonomous, exclusive, or isolated policy-making. It is policy-making on a field where mighty forces contend, forces engendered in and by society. It is policy-making subject to still other and various policy makers. Public administration is one of a number of basic political processes by which these people achieve and control government.

19. From the point of view expressed in the above paragraph, public administration is   19.____

    A. becoming a technical field with completely objective processes
    B. the primary force in modern society
    C. a technical field which should be divorced from the actual decision-making function
    D. basically anti-democratic
    E. intimately related to politics

20. According to the above paragraph, public administration is NOT entirely
    20.____

    A. a force generated in and by society
    B. subject at times to controlling influences
    C. a social process
    D. policy-making relating to administrative practices
    E. related to policy-making at lower levels

21. The above paragraph asserts that public administration
    21.____

    A. develops the basic and controlling policies
    B. is the result of policies made by many different forces
    C. should attempt to break through its isolated policymaking and engage on a broader field
    D. is a means of directing government
    E. is subject to the political processes by which acts are controlled

Questions 22-24.

DIRECTIONS: Questions 22 through 24 are to be answered SOLELY on the basis of the following paragraph.

    In order to understand completely the source of an employee's insecurity on his job, it is necessary to understand how he came to be, who he is, and what kind of a person he is away from his job. This would necessitate an understanding of those personal assets and liabilities which the employee brings to the job situation. These arise from his individual characteristics and his past experiences and established patterns of interpersonal relations. This whole area is of tremendous scope, encompassing everything included within the study of psychiatry and interpersonal relations. Therefore, it has been impracticable to consider it in detail. Attention has been focused on the relatively circumscribed area of the actual occupational situation. The factors considered – those which the employee brings to the job situation and which arise from his individual characteristics and his past experience and established patterns of interpersonal relations – are: intellectual level or capacity, specific aptitudes, education, work experience, health, social and economic background, patterns of interpersonal relations and resultant personality characteristics.

22. According to the above paragraph, the one of the following fields of study which would be of LEAST importance in the study of the problem is the
    22.____

    A. relationships existing among employees
    B. causes of employee insecurity in the job situation
    C. conflict, if it exists, between intellectual level and work experience
    D. distribution of intellectual achievement
    E. relationship between employee characteristics and the established pattern of interpersonal relations in the work situation

23. According to the above paragraph, in order to make a thoroughgoing and comprehensive study of the sources of employee insecurity, the field of study should include
    23.____

    A. only such circumscribed areas as are involved in extra-occupational situations
    B. a study of the dominant mores of the period
    C. all branches of the science of psychology

D. a determination of the characteristics, such as intellectual capacity, which an employee should bring to the job situation

E. employee personality characteristics arising from previous relationships with other people

24. It is implied by the above paragraph that it would be of GREATEST advantage to bring to this problem a comprehensive knowledge of   24.____

    A. all established patterns of interpersonal relations
    B. the milieu in which the employee group is located
    C. what assets and liabilities are presented in the job situation
    D. methods of focusing attention on relatively circumscribed regions
    E. the sources of an employee's insecurity on his job

Questions 25-26.

DIRECTIONS: Questions 25 and 26 are to be answered SOLELY on the basis of the following paragraph.

    If, during a study, some hundreds of values of a variable (such as annual number of latenesses for each employee in a department) have been noted merely in the arbitrary order in which they happen to occur, the mind cannot properly grasp the significance of the record; the observations must be ranked or classified in some way before the characteristics of the series can be comprehended, and those comparisons, on which arguments as to causation depend, can be made with other series. A dichotomous classification is too crude; if the values are merely classified according to whether they exceed or fall short of some fixed value, a large part of the information given by the original record is lost. Numerical measurements lend themselves with peculiar readiness to a manifold classification.

25. According to the above paragraph, if the values of a variable which are gathered during a study are classified in a few subdivisions, the MOST likely result will be   25.____

    A. an inability to grasp the significance of the record
    B. an inability to relate the series with other series
    C. a loss of much of the information in the original data
    D. a loss of the readiness with which numerical measurements lend themselves to a manifold classification
    E. that the order in which they happen to occur will be arbitrary

26. The above paragraph advocates, with respect to numerical data, the use of   26.____

    A. arbitrary order
    B. comparisons with other series
    C. a two value classification
    D. a many value classification
    E. all values of a variable

Question 27.

DIRECTIONS: Question 27 is to be answered SOLELY on the basis of the following paragraph.

A more significant manifestation of the concern of the community with the general welfare is the collection and dissemination of statistics. This statement may cause the reader to smile, for statistics seem to be drab and prosaic things. The great growth of statistics, however, is one of the most remarkable characteristics of the age. Never before has a community kept track from month to month, and in some cases from week to week, of how many people are born, how many die and from what causes, how many are sick, how much is being produced, how much is being sold, how many people are at work, how many people are unemployed, how long they have been out of work, what prices people pay, how much income they receive and from what sources, how much they owe, what they intend to buy. These elaborate attempts of the country to keep informed about what is happening mean that the community is concerned with how its members are faring and with the conditions under which they live. For this reason, the present age may take pride in its numerous and regular statistical reports and in the rapid increase in the number of these reports. No other age has evidenced such a keen interest in the conditions of the people.

27.   The writer implies that statistics are   27.____

    A.   too scientific for general use
    B.   too elaborate and too drab
    C.   related to the improvement of living conditions
    D.   frequently misinterpreted
    E.   a product of the machine age

KEY (CORRECT ANSWERS)

1.	E	11.	C
2.	C	12.	C
3.	A	13.	C
4.	B	14.	B
5.	A	15.	D
6.	D	16.	E
7.	A	17.	A
8.	D	18.	E
9.	B	19.	E
10.	A	20.	D

21.	D
22.	D
23.	E
24.	B
25.	C
26.	D
27.	C

ARITHMETICAL REASONING
EXAMINATION SECTION
TEST 1

DIRECTIONS: Each question or incomplete statement is followed by several suggested answers or completions. Select the one that BEST answers the question or completes the statement. *PRINT THE LETTER OF THE CORRECT ANSWER IN THE SPACE AT THE RIGHT.*

1. You have conducted a traffic survey at 10 two-lane bridges and find the traffic between 4:30 and 5:30 P.M. averages 665 cars per bridge that hour. You can't find the tabulation sheet for bridge #7, but you know that 6,066 cars were counted at the other 9 bridges. Determine from this how many must have been counted at bridge #7.   1._____

   A. 584   B. 674   C. 665   D. 607

2. You pay temporary help $8.40 per hour and regular employees $9.00 per hour. Your workload is temporarily heavy, so you need 20 hours of extra regular employees' time to catch up. If you do this on overtime, you must pay time and a half. If you use temporary help, it takes 25% more time to do the job.   2._____
   What is the DIFFERENCE in cost between the two alternatives? _____ more for

   _____ .

   A. $15; temporary   B. $30; temporary
   C. $60; regular   D. $102; regular

3. An experienced clerk can process the mailing of annual forms in 9 days. A new clerk takes 14 days to process them.   3._____
   If they work together, how many days MOST NEARLY will it take to do the processing?

   A. 4 1/2   B. 5 1/2   C. 6 1/2   D. 7

4. A certain administrative aide is usually able to successfully handle 27% of all telephone inquiries without assistance. In a particular month, he receives 1,200 inquiries and handles 340 of them successfully on his own. How many more inquiries has he handled successfully in that month than would have been expected of him based on his usual rate?   4._____

   A. 10   B. 16   C. 24   D. 44

5. A basketball team purchased uniforms from a sports shop for $1,072, less discounts of 15% and 10%.   5._____
   The check should be made out in the sum of

   A. $804.56   B. $820.08
   C. $837.72   D. none of the above

6. A secretary is entitled to 1 1/3 days of sick leave for every 32 days of work.   6._____
   How many days of work must the secretary have to her credit in order to be entitled to 12 days of sick leave?

   A. 272   B. 288   C. 290   D. 512

7. A school secretary, whose annual salary is $54,850, contributes 9.8% to the retirement   7.____
fund. Other monthly deductions from her salary are: federal income tax, $700; state
income tax, $150; social security tax, $100.
The amount of her monthly check is

   A. $3,272.90   B. $3,172.90   C. $3,174.00   D. $3,164.00

8. Suppose a review of the completed work of three operators for a certain period shows   8.____
that operator A processed 250 files and that operator B processed 285, 60 more than
operator C completed.
To find the average number of files processed by the three operators, one would need
to

   A. subtract, then add, then divide
   B. subtract, then divide
   C. add, then divide
   D. add, then divide, then subtract

9. If there are 875 files to be processed and an operator completes 320 files by herself,   9.____
what percentage of the total did she MOST NEARLY complete?

   A. 21%   B. 27%   C. 36%   D. 43%

10. An operator processed 907 files in one day. To speed the work, two other workers are   10.____
assigned, and together the three operators process 2,407 files.
The percentage of increase in the number of files processed is MOST NEARLY

   A. 155%   B. 165%   C. 175%   D. 185%

11. Two operators have processed 368 files and 175 files, respectively.   11.____
To find the difference between the number processed by each operator and to check
the accuracy of the calculations, it would be BEST to do which of the following?

   A. Add 368 to 175 to find the answer; then subtract 175 from the answer to check.
   B. Add 368 and 175, and divide the sum by two to find the answer; then add 175 and
368, and divide by two to check.
   C. Subtract 175 from 368 to find the answer; then add the answer to 175 to see if it
equals 368.
   D. Divide 368 by 175 to find the answer; then multiply the answer by 175 to see if it
equals 368.

12. Four operators were assigned to complete a project. Operator A did 2/5 of the work,   12.____
Operator B did 1/6 of the work, and Operator C did 1/3 of the work.
How much work must Operator D do to complete the project?

   A. 1/5   B. 1/6   C. 2/3   D. 1/10

13. A certain job requires that 40% of the 80 pages of a file be scanned automatically, and   13.____
the rest be copied manually by the operator.
If there are 1,250 files in the entire job, what is the TOTAL number of pages the operator must copy manually?

   A. 40,000   B. 60,000   C. 80,000   D. 100,000

14. Computer X can upload 120 processed files in an hour, while Computer Z can upload 150   14._____
processed files in the same amount of time.
The production per hour of the slower machine is what fraction of the production per
hour of the faster machine?

    A. 1/5   B. 2/3   C. 4/5   D. 5/6

15. Suppose that an operator was given the responsibility for reorganizing the files in her   15._____
office. She had 3,000 cards to file in drawers 18" long. These drawers hold 100 cards for
each 1 1/2 inches of length. In each drawer, 2" of space had to be left empty for ease of
card searching.
Of the following, the PROPER order of mathematical procedures to find the fewest
number of drawers she will need would be

    A. multiply, divide, subtract, multiply
    B. subtract, divide, multiply, divide
    C. subtract, multiply, divide, divide
    D. divide, divide, subtract, multiply

16. In arithmetic, there are frequently several ways to arrive at an answer.   16._____
Which one of the following can NOT be used to find the value of 20% of 7,372?

    A. 7,372 ÷ .2   B. 7,372 x .2
    C. 7,372 x .20   D. 1/5 of 7,372

17. A certain department submitted a payroll request for separate checks for each of 115   17._____
clerks, 52 typists, 107 technicians, 23 administrators, 12 messengers, 8 drivers, and 35
others. The average amount of each check was $327.53.
The TOTAL payroll was

    A. $113,290.46   B. $114,180.56
    C. $114,280.46   D. $115,290.56

18. A certain city administration is composed of four departments: Departments W, X, Y, and   18._____
Z. Of the personnel in this administration, 1/3 work for Department W; 1/4, for Depart-
ment X; and 1/6, for Department Y.
What part of the administration's personnel is working for Department Z?

    A. 1/4   B. 1/5   C. 1/6   D. 1/7

19. Suppose an operator finds that the first job he did one day took 35 minutes, the second   19._____
took 1/4 hour, the third 11 minutes, and the fourth took 17 minutes. Between each job,
there was a ten-minute period for record keeping.
If he began the first job at 9:15 A.M., at what time did he FINISH the fourth job?

    A. 10:33 A.M.   B. 10:53 A.M.
    C. 11:03 A.M.   D. 11:13 A.M.

20. A certain program can process a maximum of 1,000 files per minute. However, this pro-   20._____
gram is not run all the time, and not every batch of files is as large as 1,000. In the first
five minutes of an hour, 3,000 files were processed; in the next five minutes, 200 were
processed; and in the third five minutes, 600 were processed.
What is the RATIO of actual output of files to maximum possible output of files during
this period?

    A. 1:4   B. 3:10   C. 35:100   D. 4:10

21. A check of the time records of a certain employee reveals that he spent 9 days on sick leave last year. This employee works a 7-hour day.
The average number of hours he was on sick leave each month last year was MOST NEARLY

    A. 1 1/3   B. 5 1/4   C. 9 3/4   D. 12 1/2

21.____

22. In the same amount of time, Machine B can process only 2/3 as many files as Machine A, but 1 1/4 times as many cards as Machine C.
If Machine A can process 1,500 files per minute, how many files per minute can Machine C process?

    A. 600   B. 800   C. 1,000   D. 1,200

22.____

23. Look at the incomplete balance sheet below.

23.____

Balance Sheet

	Assets		Liabilities
A	$195,679.42	D	$378,429.58
B	$241,382.15	E	_____
C	$486,723.69		
Total		Total	

If total assets equaled total liabilities, what amount should be shown next to entry E?

    A. $545,355.68   B. $555,355.68
    C. $545,455.68   D. $555,455.68

24. Computer A can process 900 files a minute while Computer B can process 800 files a minute.
At this rate, how much LONGER would it take Computer B to process 36,000 files than it would take Computer A to process them? _____ minutes.

    A. 3   B. 5   C. 7   D. 9

24.____

25. An operator wants to find out what 47% of a certain payroll is, and then check his answer.
Of the following, the steps he should take are:

    A. Divide the amount of the payroll by .47 and multiply the answer by .47
    B. Divide .47 by the amount of the payroll and multiply the answer by the amount of the payroll
    C. Multiply the amount of the payroll by .47 and multiply the answer by .47
    D. Multiply the amount of the payroll by .47 and divide the answer by the amount of the payroll

25.____

KEY (CORRECT ANSWERS)

1.	A		11.	C
2.	C		12.	D
3.	B		13.	B
4.	B		14.	C
5.	B		15.	B
6.	B		16.	A
7.	B		17.	D
8.	A		18.	A
9.	C		19.	C
10.	B		20.	A

21.	B
22.	B
23.	A
24.	B
25.	D

———

SOLUTIONS TO PROBLEMS

1. (665)(10) - 6066 = 584 cases

2. Using regular employees, the cost = (20)($9.00)(1.5) = $270 Using temporary help, the cost = (20)(1.25)($8.40) = $210 So, regular employees will cost $60 more than temporary help

3. Let x = number of days. Then, (1/9)(x) + (1/14)(x) = 1. Thus, 14x + 9x = 126. Solving, x = 126/23 = 5 1/2 days

4. 340 - (.27)(1200) = 16 inquiries

5. ($1072)(.85)(.90) = $820.08

6. 12 ÷ 1 1/3 = 9. Then, (9)(32) = 288 days of work

7. Her monthly check = $4570.83 - (.098)($4570.83) - $700 - $150 - $100 ≈ $3172.90

8. First, subtract 60 from 285 to get 225. Then, add: 250, 285, and 225 to get 760. Finally, divide 760 by 3 to get 253 1/3

9. 320/875 ≈ 37% (Selection C is closest with 36%)

10. (2407-907) ÷ 907 ≈ 165%

11. First subtract 175 from 368 to get 193. Second, to check this answer, add 193 to 175.

12. Operator D did $1 - \dfrac{2}{5} - \dfrac{1}{6} - \dfrac{1}{3} = \dfrac{1}{10}$

13. (.60)(80)(1250) = 60,000 pages

14. 120/150 = 4/5

15. Subtract: 18" - 2" = 16"; divide: 16" 1 1/2" = $10.\overline{6}$, rounded down to 10; multiply: (10)(100) = 1000 cards per drawer.
Finally, divide: 3000 ÷ 1000 = 3 drawers

16. 20% of 7372 = 1474.4 ≠ 7372 ÷ .2, which is 36,860

17. Total payroll = ($327.53)(115+52+107+23+12+8+35) = $115,290.56

18. $1 - \dfrac{1}{3} - \dfrac{1}{4} - \dfrac{1}{6} = \dfrac{1}{4}$ working for Department Z

19. Time between beginning of 1st job to end of 4th job = 35 + 10 + 15 + 10 + 11 + 10 + 17 = 108 min. = 1 hr. 48 min. Then, 9:15 AM + 1 hr. 48 min. = 11:03 AM

20. Maximum output in 15 min. = (1000)(15) = 15,000 files. Actual output in 15 min. = 3000 + 200 + 600 = 3800 files Then, 3800 ÷ 15,000 = 19:75, which is closest to 1:4

21. (9)(7) = 63 hours per year = 5 1/4 hours per month

22. Machine B can process (2/3) (1500) = 1000 cards per min., so Machine C can process 1000 ÷ 1 1/4 = 800 cards per min.

23. Entry E = Entry A + Entry B + Entry C - Entry D = $545,355.68

24. 36,000/800 - 36,000/900 = 5 min.

25. Multiply the payroll by .47. To check, take answer obtained and divide by payroll amount. (Should get .47)

TEST 2

DIRECTIONS: Each question or incomplete statement is followed by several suggested
answers or completions. Select the one that BEST answers the question or
completes the statement. *PRINT THE LETTER OF THE CORRECT ANSWER
IN THE SPACE AT THE RIGHT.*

1.   3/4 of 1 percent expressed as a decimal is   1._____

   A.   7.5   B.   .75   C.   .075   D.   .0075

2.   If one telephone operator can handle 50 calls in 6 minutes and another can take care of   2._____
     the same number in 3 minutes, then both working together can dispose of the 50 calls in
     _____ minute(s).

   A.   1/2   B.   1   C.   1 1/2   D.   2

3.   If an operator sells two cars at $6,000 each, making a profit of 20 percent on one and   3._____
     taking a loss of 20 percent on the other, then, on the whole transaction involving the pur-
     chase and sale of the two cars, she will

   A.   break even   B.   gain $500
   C.   lose $500   D.   do none of the above

4.   If X percent of the length of telephone wire A is equal to Y percent of the length of tele-   4._____
     phone wire B, and telephone wire B measures Z feet, then the length of telephone wire
     A, expressed in feet, is

   A.   YZ/X   B.   100XY   C.   100Z/XY   D.   100YZ/X

5.   If there were 107,147 employees in all classes of the city service, and 629 of these were   5._____
     in the exempt class, then the percentage of city employees in the exempt class was
     MOST NEARLY _____ percent.

   A.   1/4 of 1   B.   1/2 of 1   C.   3/4 of 1   D.   1

6.   The sum of 90.79, 79.09, 97.90, and 9.97 is   6._____

   A.   277.75   B.   278.56   C.   276.94   D.   277.93

7.   A cube-shaped box has a side of S inches. The volume of the box is S^3 cubic inches.   7._____
     If each side of the box were increased by 3 inches, the volume would then be repre-
     sented by

   A. $(S+3)^3$ B. S^3+3 C. $(3S+9)^3$ D. S^3+3^3

8.   In an agency, 7/12 of the employees are engaged in clerical work, 1/3 of the employees   8._____
     are engaged in supervisory work, and 1/4 of the employees are not engaged in either
     clerical or supervisory work.
     How many employees in this agency are engaged in BOTH clerical and supervisory
     work?

   A.   1/6   B.   1/12   C.   1/3   D.   1/4

9. A new computer installation has the memory capacity to run 15 jobs simultaneously, whereas the old computer installation has the memory capacity to run 5 jobs simultaneously.
   If it took the old computer 2 hours and 36 minutes to run 250 jobs, how long will it take the new computer to run 625 jobs, assuming it takes the same amount of time for both computers to run each single job?

   A. 52 minutes
   B. 1 hour 30 minutes
   C. 1 hour 50 minutes
   D. 2 hours 10 minutes

9._____

10. In a right triangle, the area is equal to 1/2 the product of two legs. Assume you have the following five right triangles with legs as indicated:
   Triangle I   legs 9 inches and 7 inches long
   Triangle II   legs 8 inches and 8 inches long
   Triangle III   legs 3 inches and 13 inches long
   Triangle IV   legs 5 inches and 12 inches long
   Triangle V   legs 4 inches and 16 inches long
   Which of the above triangles have the SAME area?

   A. I and II   B. III and IV   C. I and V   D. II and V

10._____

11. Due to a nationwide fuel shortage, the speed limit on a major highway was lowered 5 miles per hour. Assume that a certain motorist always drives at the legal speed limit. If he were able to drive 99 miles in 2 1/5 hours at the original speed limit, how long will it take him to drive 100 miles at the new speed limit?
   2 hours _____ minutes.

   A. 12   B. 20   C. 30   D. 50

11._____

12. If the pressure (P) of a gas in a closed container varies directly with the temperature (T) and inversely with the volume (V) of the container, which of the following is TRUE?
   If the

   A. temperature is increased, the volume is increased
   B. pressure is decreased, the temperature is increased
   C. volume is increased, the pressure is increased
   D. temperature is increased, the pressure is increased

12._____

13. An operator processes an average of 75 files an hour for a normal work day of 7 hours. If 20% of the files must be verified, how many of the operator's files must be verified in a normal 5-day work week?

   A. 115   B. 263   C. 525   D. 2,625

13._____

14. If the Law of Division applying to exponents states that $X^m \div X^n = X^{m-n}$, what does $2^6 \div 2^4$ equal?

   A. 1   B. 4   C. 8   D. 16

14._____

15. In one state, the tax rate on the purchase price of an automobile is 3% higher than the tax rate in a neighboring state. The base price of the automobile is $3,000 in both states. If the automobile costs $3,120 in the state with the lower tax rate, what does it cost in the state with the higher tax rate?

   A. $3,120   B. $3,210   C. $3,300   D. $3,936

15._____

16. An employee earns $120 a day and works 5 days a week. He will earn $5,400 in _____ weeks.

    A. 5   B. 7   C. 8   D. 9

16._____

17. In a certain bureau, the entire staff consists of 1 senior supervisor, 2 supervisors, 6 assistant supervisors, and 54 associate workers.
The percent of the staff who are NOT associate workers is MOST NEARLY

    A. 14%   B. 21%   C. 27%   D. 32%

17._____

18. In a certain bureau, five employees each earn $2,500 a month, another 3 employees each earn $3,000 a month, and another two employees each earn $3,500 a month.
The monthly payroll for these employees is

    A. $9,000   B. $22,000   C. $28,500   D. $30,000

18._____

19. An employee contributes 5% of his salary to the pension fund.
If his salary is $3,000 a month, the amount of his contribution to the pension fund in a year is

    A. $1,200   B. $1,800   C. $2,400   D. $3,000

19._____

20. The number of square feet in an area that is 50 feet long and 30 feet wide is

    A. 80   B. 150   C. 800   D. 1,500

20._____

21. The sum of 5 1/2, 4, 3 1/4, and 2 is

    A. 14 3/4   B. 13 1/2   C. 12   D. 10 1/4

21._____

22. The sum of 2.6", 1.2", and 4.1" is

    A. 6.6"   B. 7.3"   C. 7.9"   D. 8.2"

22._____

23. The fraction 3/8 expressed as a decimal is

    A. 0.250   B. 0.281   C. 0.375   D. 0.406

23._____

24. The sum of 2' 6", 0' 3", and 3' 1" is

    A. 2' 9"   B. 5' 7"   C. 5' 10"   D. 15' 0"

24._____

25. A man and boy working together complete a job in 8 hours. If a boy does half as much work as a man, two men working together can complete the job in _____ hours.

    A. 7 1/2   B. 7   C. 6 1/2   D. 6

25._____

KEY (CORRECT ANSWERS)

1.	D		11.	C
2.	D		12.	D
3.	C		13.	C
4.	A		14.	B
5.	B		15.	B
6.	A		16.	D
7.	A		17.	A
8.	A		18.	C
9.	D		19.	B
10.	D		20.	D

21.	A
22.	C
23.	C
24.	C
25.	D

SOLUTIONS TO PROBLEMS

1. 3/4 of 1% = (.75)(.01) = .0075

2. Let x = required min. Then, $(\frac{1}{6})(x) + (\frac{1}{3})(x) = 1$. Simplifying, Solving, x = 2

3. Her cost for the 2 vehicles = ($6000 ÷ 1.20) + ($6000 ÷ .80) = $5000 + $7500 = $12,500. Since she sold the 2 vehicles for $12,000, she lost $500.

4. Let L = length of wire A. Then, $(\frac{x}{100})(L) = (\frac{Y}{100})(Z)$.

   Solving, $L = (\frac{Y}{100})(Z)(\frac{100}{x}) = YZ/X$

5. 629 ÷ 107,147 .006, which is closest to 1/2 of 1 percent

6. 90.79 + 79.09 + 97.90 + 9.97 = 277.75

7. Each new side is s+3 inches. New volume = $(s+3)^3$ cubic inches

8. Let x = fraction of employees required in both categories.

   Then, $\frac{7}{12} + \frac{1}{3} + \frac{1}{4} - x = 1$. Solving, $x = \frac{1}{6}$

9. To run 250 jobs, the new computer needs (1/3)(156) = 52 min. So, to run 625 jobs, the new computer would need (625/250)(52) = 130 min. = 2 hrs. 10 min.

10. The areas of triangles I, II, III, IV, V are (in square inches) 31 1/2, 32, 19 1/2, 30, and 32, respectively. Thus, triangles II and V have the same area.

11. $99 ÷ 2\frac{1}{5} = 45$ mph. The new speed limit is 40 mph, so 100 miles takes 100/40 = 2.5 hrs. = 2 hrs. 30 min.

12. We can write P = KT/V, where K is a constant. If the volume remains constant, then as temperature is increased, the pressure is increased.

13. (75)(7)(5)(.20) = 525 cards to be verified

14. $2^6 ÷ 2^4 = 2^2 = 4$

15. ($3120-$3000) ÷ $3000 = 4%. So, the tax rate in the other state is 7%. Auto cost = ($3000)(1.07) = $3210

16. ($120)(5) = $600 per week. Then, $5400 ÷ $600 = 9 weeks

6 (#2)

17. $(1+2+6)/63 \approx 14\%$

18. $(5)(\$2500) + (3)(\$3000) + (2)(\$3500) = \$28,500$

19. $(\$3000)(12)(.05) = \$1800$ pension contribution in a year.

20. $(50')(30') = 1500$ sq.ft.

21. $5\ 1/2 + 4 + 3\ 1/4 + 2 = 14\ 3/4$

22. $2.6" + 1.2" + 4.1" = 7.9"$

23. $3/8 = .375$

24. $2'\ 6" + 0'\ 3" + 3'\ 1" = 5'\ 10"$

25. A man and a boy = 1 1/2 men working 8 hrs. = 12 man-hours
Then, $12 \div 2 = 6$ hours

ARITHMETICAL REASONING
EXAMINATION SECTION
TEST 1

DIRECTIONS: Each question or incomplete statement is followed by several suggested answers or completions. Select the one that BEST answers the question or completes the statement. *PRINT THE LETTER OF THE CORRECT ANSWER IN THE SPACE AT THE RIGHT.*

1. You have conducted a traffic survey at 10 two-lane bridges and find the traffic between 4:30 and 5:30 P.M. averages 665 cars per bridge that hour. You can't find the tabulation sheet for bridge #7, but you know that 6,066 cars were counted at the other 9 bridges. Determine from this how many must have been counted at bridge #7. 1.____

    A. 584   B. 674   C. 665   D. 607

2. You pay temporary help $8.40 per hour and regular employees $9.00 per hour. Your workload is temporarily heavy, so you need 20 hours of extra regular employees' time to catch up. If you do this on overtime, you must pay time and a half. If you use temporary help, it takes 25% more time to do the job.
What is the DIFFERENCE in cost between the two alternatives? _____ more for

_____ . 2.____

    A. $15; temporary   B. $30; temporary
    C. $60; regular   D. $102; regular

3. An experienced clerk can process the mailing of annual forms in 9 days. A new clerk takes 14 days to process them.
If they work together, how many days MOST NEARLY will it take to do the processing? 3.____

    A. 4 1/2   B. 5 1/2   C. 6 1/2   D. 7

4. A certain administrative aide is usually able to successfully handle 27% of all telephone inquiries without assistance. In a particular month, he receives 1,200 inquiries and handles 340 of them successfully on his own. How many more inquiries has he handled successfully in that month than would have been expected of him based on his usual rate? 4.____

    A. 10   B. 16   C. 24   D. 44

5. A basketball team purchased uniforms from a sports shop for $1,072, less discounts of 15% and 10%.
The check should be made out in the sum of 5.____

    A. $804.56   B. $820.08
    C. $837.72   D. none of the above

6. A secretary is entitled to 1 1/3 days of sick leave for every 32 days of work.
How many days of work must the secretary have to her credit in order to be entitled to 12 days of sick leave? 6.____

    A. 272   B. 288   C. 290   D. 512

7. A school secretary, whose annual salary is $54,850, contributes 9.8% to the retirement fund. Other monthly deductions from her salary are: federal income tax, $700; state income tax, $150; social security tax, $100.
The amount of her monthly check is

    A. $3,272.90   B. $3,172.90   C. $3,174.00   D. $3,164.00

7.____

8. Suppose a review of the completed work of three operators for a certain period shows that operator A processed 250 files and that operator B processed 285, 60 more than operator C completed.
To find the average number of files processed by the three operators, one would need to

    A. subtract, then add, then divide
    B. subtract, then divide
    C. add, then divide
    D. add, then divide, then subtract

8.____

9. If there are 875 files to be processed and an operator completes 320 files by herself, what percentage of the total did she MOST NEARLY complete?

    A. 21%   B. 27%   C. 36%   D. 43%

9.____

10. An operator processed 907 files in one day. To speed the work, two other workers are assigned, and together the three operators process 2,407 files.
The percentage of increase in the number of files processed is MOST NEARLY

    A. 155%   B. 165%   C. 175%   D. 185%

10.____

11. Two operators have processed 368 files and 175 files, respectively.
To find the difference between the number processed by each operator and to check the accuracy of the calculations, it would be BEST to do which of the following?

    A. Add 368 to 175 to find the answer; then subtract 175 from the answer to check.
    B. Add 368 and 175, and divide the sum by two to find the answer; then add 175 and 368, and divide by two to check.
    C. Subtract 175 from 368 to find the answer; then add the answer to 175 to see if it equals 368.
    D. Divide 368 by 175 to find the answer; then multiply the answer by 175 to see if it equals 368.

11.____

12. Four operators were assigned to complete a project. Operator A did 2/5 of the work, Operator B did 1/6 of the work, and Operator C did 1/3 of the work.
How much work must Operator D do to complete the project?

    A. 1/5   B. 1/6   C. 2/3   D. 1/10

12.____

13. A certain job requires that 40% of the 80 pages of a file be scanned automatically, and the rest be copied manually by the operator.
If there are 1,250 files in the entire job, what is the TOTAL number of pages the operator must copy manually?

    A. 40,000   B. 60,000   C. 80,000   D. 100,000

13.____

14. Computer X can upload 120 processed files in an hour, while Computer Z can upload 150 processed files in the same amount of time.
The production per hour of the slower machine is what fraction of the production per hour of the faster machine?

   A. 1/5   B. 2/3   C. 4/5   D. 5/6   14._____

15. Suppose that an operator was given the responsibility for reorganizing the files in her office. She had 3,000 cards to file in drawers 18" long. These drawers hold 100 cards for each 1 1/2 inches of length. In each drawer, 2" of space had to be left empty for ease of card searching.
Of the following, the PROPER order of mathematical procedures to find the fewest number of drawers she will need would be   15._____

   A. multiply, divide, subtract, multiply
   B. subtract, divide, multiply, divide
   C. subtract, multiply, divide, divide
   D. divide, divide, subtract, multiply

16. In arithmetic, there are frequently several ways to arrive at an answer.
Which one of the following can NOT be used to find the value of 20% of 7,372?   16._____

   A. 7,372 ÷ .2   B. 7,372 x .2
   C. 7,372 x .20   D. 1/5 of 7,372

17. A certain department submitted a payroll request for separate checks for each of 115 clerks, 52 typists, 107 technicians, 23 administrators, 12 messengers, 8 drivers, and 35 others. The average amount of each check was $327.53.
The TOTAL payroll was   17._____

   A. $113,290.46   B. $114,180.56
   C. $114,280.46   D. $115,290.56

18. A certain city administration is composed of four departments: Departments W, X, Y, and Z. Of the personnel in this administration, 1/3 work for Department W; 1/4, for Department X; and 1/6, for Department Y.
What part of the administration's personnel is working for Department Z?   18._____

   A. 1/4   B. 1/5   C. 1/6   D. 1/7

19. Suppose an operator finds that the first job he did one day took 35 minutes, the second took 1/4 hour, the third 11 minutes, and the fourth took 17 minutes. Between each job, there was a ten-minute period for record keeping.
If he began the first job at 9:15 A.M., at what time did he FINISH the fourth job?   19._____

   A. 10:33 A.M.   B. 10:53 A.M.
   C. 11:03 A.M.   D. 11:13 A.M.

20. A certain program can process a maximum of 1,000 files per minute. However, this program is not run all the time, and not every batch of files is as large as 1,000. In the first five minutes of an hour, 3,000 files were processed; in the next five minutes, 200 were processed; and in the third five minutes, 600 were processed.
What is the RATIO of actual output of files to maximum possible output of files during this period?   20._____

   A. 1:4   B. 3:10   C. 35:100   D. 4:10

21. A check of the time records of a certain employee reveals that he spent 9 days on sick 21.____
leave last year. This employee works a 7-hour day.
The average number of hours he was on sick leave each month last year was MOST
NEARLY

    A. 1 1/3   B. 5 1/4   C. 9 3/4   D. 12 1/2

22. In the same amount of time, Machine B can process only 2/3 as many files as Machine 22.____
A, but 1 1/4 times as many cards as Machine C.
If Machine A can process 1,500 files per minute, how many files per minute can
Machine C process?

    A. 600   B. 800   C. 1,000   D. 1,200

23. Look at the incomplete balance sheet below. 23.____

Balance Sheet

	Assets		Liabilities
A	$195,679.42	D	$378,429.58
B	$241,382.15	E	_____
C	$486,723.69		
Total		Total	

If total assets equaled total liabilities, what amount should be shown next to entry E?

    A. $545,355.68   B. $555,355.68
    C. $545,455.68   D. $555,455.68

24. Computer A can process 900 files a minute while Computer B can process 800 files a 24.____
minute.
At this rate, how much LONGER would it take Computer B to process 36,000 files than
it would take Computer A to process them? _____ minutes.

    A. 3   B. 5   C. 7   D. 9

25. An operator wants to find out what 47% of a certain payroll is, and then check his answer. 25.____
Of the following, the steps he should take are:

    A. Divide the amount of the payroll by .47 and multiply the answer by .47
    B. Divide .47 by the amount of the payroll and multiply the answer by the amount of
        the payroll
    C. Multiply the amount of the payroll by .47 and multiply the answer by .47
    D. Multiply the amount of the payroll by .47 and divide the answer by the amount of
        the payroll

———————

KEY (CORRECT ANSWERS)

1.	A		11.	C
2.	C		12.	D
3.	B		13.	B
4.	B		14.	C
5.	B		15.	B
6.	B		16.	A
7.	B		17.	D
8.	A		18.	A
9.	C		19.	C
10.	B		20.	A

21.	B
22.	B
23.	A
24.	B
25.	D

SOLUTIONS TO PROBLEMS

1. (665)(10) - 6066 = 584 cases

2. Using regular employees, the cost = (20)($9.00)(1.5) = $270 Using temporary help, the cost = (20)(1.25)($8.40) = $210 So, regular employees will cost $60 more than temporary help

3. Let x = number of days. Then, $(1/9)(x) + (1/14)(x) = 1$. Thus, $14x + 9x = 126$. Solving, $x = 126/23 = 5\ 1/2$ days

4. 340 - (.27)(1200) = 16 inquiries

5. ($1072)(.85)(.90) = $820.08

6. $12 \div 1\ 1/3 = 9$. Then, (9)(32) = 288 days of work

7. Her monthly check = $4570.83 - (.098)($4570.83) - $700 - $150 - $100 $\approx$ $3172.90

8. First, subtract 60 from 285 to get 225. Then, add: 250, 285, and 225 to get 760. Finally, divide 760 by 3 to get 253 1/3

9. $320/875 \approx 37\%$ (Selection C is closest with 36%)

10. $(2407-907) \div 907 \approx 165\%$

11. First subtract 175 from 368 to get 193. Second, to check this answer, add 193 to 175.

12. Operator D did $1 - \dfrac{2}{5} - \dfrac{1}{6} - \dfrac{1}{3} = \dfrac{1}{10}$

13. (.60)(80)(1250) = 60,000 pages

14. 120/150 = 4/5

15. Subtract: 18" - 2" = 16"; divide: 16" 1 1/2" = $10.\overline{6}$, rounded down to 10; multiply: (10)(100) = 1000 cards per drawer.
Finally, divide: $3000 \div 1000 = 3$ drawers

16. 20% of 7372 = 1474.4 $\neq$ $7372 \div .2$, which is 36,860

17. Total payroll = ($327.53)(115+52+107+23+12+8+35) = $115,290.56

18. $1 - \dfrac{1}{3} - \dfrac{1}{4} - \dfrac{1}{6} = \dfrac{1}{4}$ working for Department Z

19. Time between beginning of 1st job to end of 4th job = 35 + 10 + 15 + 10 + 11 + 10 + 17 = 108 min. = 1 hr. 48 min. Then, 9:15 AM + 1 hr. 48 min. = 11:03 AM

20. Maximum output in 15 min. = (1000)(15) = 15,000 files. Actual output in 15 min. = 3000 + 200 + 600 = 3800 files Then, $3800 \div 15,000 = 19{:}75$, which is closest to 1:4

21. (9)(7) = 63 hours per year = 5 1/4 hours per month

22. Machine B can process (2/3) (1500) = 1000 cards per min., so Machine C can process 1000 ÷ 1 1/4 = 800 cards per min.

23. Entry E = Entry A + Entry B + Entry C - Entry D = $545,355.68

24. 36,000/800 - 36,000/900 = 5 min.

25. Multiply the payroll by .47. To check, take answer obtained and divide by payroll amount. (Should get .47)

———

TEST 2

DIRECTIONS: Each question or incomplete statement is followed by several suggested answers or completions. Select the one that BEST answers the question or completes the statement. *PRINT THE LETTER OF THE CORRECT ANSWER IN THE SPACE AT THE RIGHT.*

1. 3/4 of 1 percent expressed as a decimal is

   A. 7.5   B. .75   C. .075   D. .0075

1.____

2. If one telephone operator can handle 50 calls in 6 minutes and another can take care of the same number in 3 minutes, then both working together can dispose of the 50 calls in _____ minute(s).

   A. 1/2   B. 1   C. 1 1/2   D. 2

2.____

3. If an operator sells two cars at $6,000 each, making a profit of 20 percent on one and taking a loss of 20 percent on the other, then, on the whole transaction involving the purchase and sale of the two cars, she will

   A. break even   B. gain $500
   C. lose $500   D. do none of the above

3.____

4. If X percent of the length of telephone wire A is equal to Y percent of the length of telephone wire B, and telephone wire B measures Z feet, then the length of telephone wire A, expressed in feet, is

   A. YZ/X   B. 100XY   C. 100Z/XY   D. 100YZ/X

4.____

5. If there were 107,147 employees in all classes of the city service, and 629 of these were in the exempt class, then the percentage of city employees in the exempt class was MOST NEARLY _____ percent.

   A. 1/4 of 1   B. 1/2 of 1   C. 3/4 of 1   D. 1

5.____

6. The sum of 90.79, 79.09, 97.90, and 9.97 is

   A. 277.75   B. 278.56   C. 276.94   D. 277.93

6.____

7. A cube-shaped box has a side of S inches. The volume of the box is S^3 cubic inches. If each side of the box were increased by 3 inches, the volume would then be represented by

   A. $(S+3)^3$ B. S^3+3 C. $(3S+9)^3$ D. S^3+3^3

7.____

8. In an agency, 7/12 of the employees are engaged in clerical work, 1/3 of the employees are engaged in supervisory work, and 1/4 of the employees are not engaged in either clerical or supervisory work.
How many employees in this agency are engaged in BOTH clerical and supervisory work?

   A. 1/6   B. 1/12   C. 1/3   D. 1/4

8.____

9. A new computer installation has the memory capacity to run 15 jobs simultaneously, whereas the old computer installation has the memory capacity to run 5 jobs simultaneously.
If it took the old computer 2 hours and 36 minutes to run 250 jobs, how long will it take the new computer to run 625 jobs, assuming it takes the same amount of time for both computers to run each single job?

    A. 52 minutes   B. 1 hour 30 minutes
    C. 1 hour 50 minutes   D. 2 hours 10 minutes

9.____

10. In a right triangle, the area is equal to 1/2 the product of two legs. Assume you have the following five right triangles with legs as indicated:

    Triangle I   legs 9 inches and 7 inches long
    Triangle II   legs 8 inches and 8 inches long
    Triangle III   legs 3 inches and 13 inches long
    Triangle IV   legs 5 inches and 12 inches long
    Triangle V   legs 4 inches and 16 inches long
Which of the above triangles have the SAME area?

    A. I and II   B. III and IV   C. I and V   D. II and V

10.____

11. Due to a nationwide fuel shortage, the speed limit on a major highway was lowered 5 miles per hour. Assume that a certain motorist always drives at the legal speed limit. If he were able to drive 99 miles in 2 1/5 hours at the original speed limit, how long will it take him to drive 100 miles at the new speed limit?
2 hours _____ minutes.

    A. 12   B. 20   C. 30   D. 50

11.____

12. If the pressure (P) of a gas in a closed container varies directly with the temperature (T) and inversely with the volume (V) of the container, which of the following is TRUE?
If the

    A. temperature is increased, the volume is increased
    B. pressure is decreased, the temperature is increased
    C. volume is increased, the pressure is increased
    D. temperature is increased, the pressure is increased

12.____

13. An operator processes an average of 75 files an hour for a normal work day of 7 hours. If 20% of the files must be verified, how many of the operator's files must be verified in a normal 5-day work week?

    A. 115   B. 263   C. 525   D. 2,625

13.____

14. If the Law of Division applying to exponents states that $X^m \div X^n = X^{m-n}$, what does $2^6 \div 2^4$ equal?

    A. 1   B. 4   C. 8   D. 16

14.____

15. In one state, the tax rate on the purchase price of an automobile is 3% higher than the tax rate in a neighboring state. The base price of the automobile is $3,000 in both states. If the automobile costs $3,120 in the state with the lower tax rate, what does it cost in the state with the higher tax rate?

    A. $3,120   B. $3,210   C. $3,300   D. $3,936

15.____

16. An employee earns $120 a day and works 5 days a week. He will earn $5,400 in _____ weeks. 16.____

    A. 5   B. 7   C. 8   D. 9

17. In a certain bureau, the entire staff consists of 1 senior supervisor, 2 supervisors, 6 assistant supervisors, and 54 associate workers. 17.____
    The percent of the staff who are NOT associate workers is MOST NEARLY

    A. 14%   B. 21%   C. 27%   D. 32%

18. In a certain bureau, five employees each earn $2,500 a month, another 3 employees each earn $3,000 a month, and another two employees each earn $3,500 a month. 18.____
    The monthly payroll for these employees is

    A. $9,000   B. $22,000   C. $28,500   D. $30,000

19. An employee contributes 5% of his salary to the pension fund. 19.____
    If his salary is $3,000 a month, the amount of his contribution to the pension fund in a year is

    A. $1,200   B. $1,800   C. $2,400   D. $3,000

20. The number of square feet in an area that is 50 feet long and 30 feet wide is 20.____

    A. 80   B. 150   C. 800   D. 1,500

21. The sum of 5 1/2, 4, 3 1/4, and 2 is 21.____

    A. 14 3/4   B. 13 1/2   C. 12   D. 10 1/4

22. The sum of 2.6", 1.2", and 4.1" is 22.____

    A. 6.6"   B. 7.3"   C. 7.9"   D. 8.2"

23. The fraction 3/8 expressed as a decimal is 23.____

    A. 0.250   B. 0.281   C. 0.375   D. 0.406

24. The sum of 2' 6", 0' 3", and 3' 1" is 24.____

    A. 2' 9"   B. 5' 7"   C. 5' 10"   D. 15' 0"

25. A man and boy working together complete a job in 8 hours. If a boy does half as much work as a man, two men working together can complete the job in _____ hours. 25.____

    A. 7 1/2   B. 7   C. 6 1/2   D. 6

KEY (CORRECT ANSWERS)

1.	D		11.	C
2.	D		12.	D
3.	C		13.	C
4.	A		14.	B
5.	B		15.	B
6.	A		16.	D
7.	A		17.	A
8.	A		18.	C
9.	D		19.	B
10.	D		20.	D

21.	A
22.	C
23.	C
24.	C
25.	D

___

5 (#2)

SOLUTIONS TO PROBLEMS

1. 3/4 of 1% = (.75)(.01) = .0075

2. Let x = required min. Then, $(\frac{1}{6})(x) + (\frac{1}{3})(x) = 1$. Simplifying, Solving, x = 2

3. Her cost for the 2 vehicles = ($6000 ÷ 1.20) + ($6000 ÷ .80) = $5000 + $7500 = $12,500. Since she sold the 2 vehicles for $12,000, she lost $500.

4. Let L = length of wire A. Then, $(\frac{x}{100})(L) = (\frac{Y}{100})(Z)$.

   Solving, $L = (\frac{Y}{100})(Z)(\frac{100}{x}) = YZ/X$

5. 629 ÷ 107,147 .006, which is closest to 1/2 of 1 percent

6. 90.79 + 79.09 + 97.90 + 9.97 = 277.75

7. Each new side is s+3 inches. New volume = $(s+3)^3$ cubic inches

8. Let x = fraction of employees required in both categories.

   Then, $\frac{7}{12} + \frac{1}{3} + \frac{1}{4} \cdot x = 1$. Solving, $x = \frac{1}{6}$

9. To run 250 jobs, the new computer needs (1/3)(156) = 52 min.
   So, to run 625 jobs, the new computer would need (625/250)(52) = 130 min. = 2 hrs. 10 min.

10. The areas of triangles I, II, III, IV, V are (in square inches) 31 1/2, 32, 19 1/2, 30, and 32, respectively. Thus, triangles II and V have the same area.

11. $99 ÷ 2\frac{1}{5} = 45$ mph. The new speed limit is 40 mph, so 100 miles takes 100/40 = 2.5 hrs. = 2 hrs. 30 min.

12. We can write P = KT/V, where K is a constant. If the volume remains constant, then as temperature is increased, the pressure is increased.

13. (75)(7)(5)(.20) = 525 cards to be verified

14. $2^6 ÷ 2^4 = 2^2 = 4$

15. ($3120-$3000) ÷ $3000 = 4%. So, the tax rate in the other state is 7%. Auto cost = ($3000)(1.07) = $3210

16. ($120)(5) = $600 per week. Then, $5400 ÷ $600 = 9 weeks

17. $(1+2+6)/63 \approx 14\%$

18. $(5)(\$2500) + (3)(\$3000) + (2)(\$3500) = \$28,500$

19. $(\$3000)(12)(.05) = \$1800$ pension contribution in a year.

20. $(50')(30') = 1500$ sq.ft.

21. $5\ 1/2 + 4 + 3\ 1/4 + 2 = 14\ 3/4$

22. $2.6" + 1.2" + 4.1" = 7.9"$

23. $3/8 = .375$

24. $2'\ 6" + 0'\ 3" + 3'\ 1" = 5'\ 10"$

25. A man and a boy = 1 1/2 men working 8 hrs. = 12 man-hours
Then, $12 \div 2 = 6$ hours

FLOWCHARTING

When you program a computer, you must first think through what you want to get done. It is necessary to take small organized steps. The ordering of your thoughts is called an *algorithm.* It is a step-by-step process to complete a certain task.

For instance, imagine that you are looking for a new job. You need a plan of action. Your algorithm:

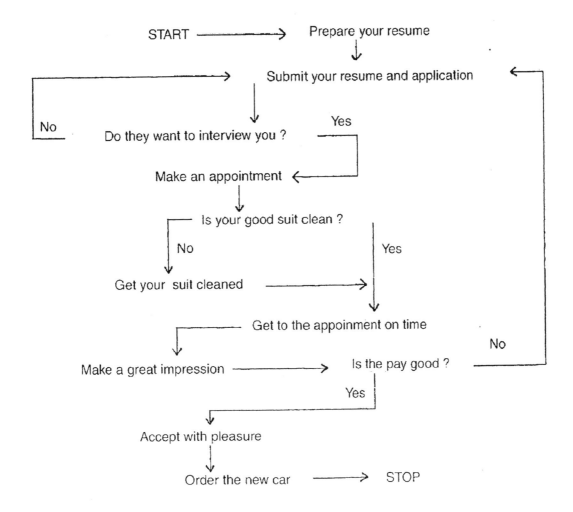

This is the flowchart that goes with your algorithm. Compare them. Note the use of shapes for each step. These are symbols.

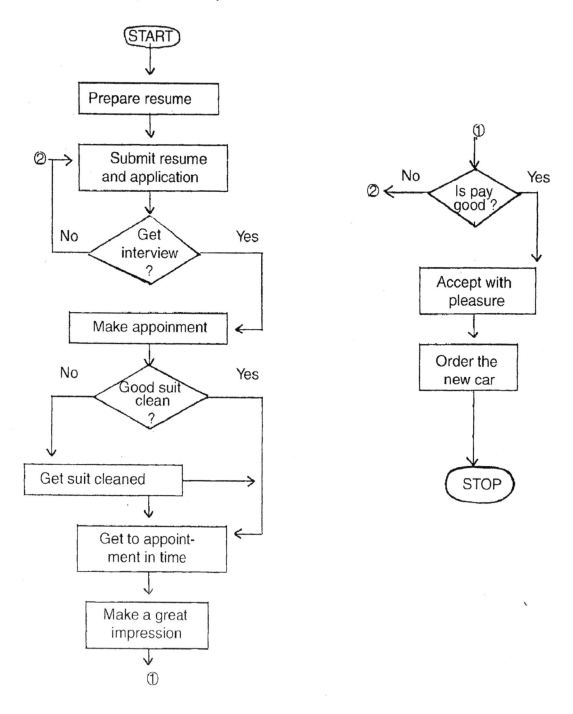

3

FLOWCHART SYMBOLS make flowcharts uniform and easier to read:

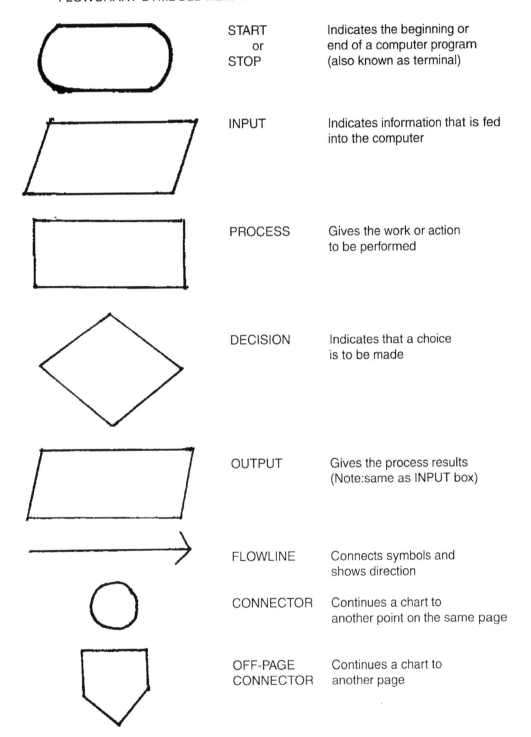

START
or
STOP — Indicates the beginning or end of a computer program (also known as terminal)

INPUT — Indicates information that is fed into the computer

PROCESS — Gives the work or action to be performed

DECISION — Indicates that a choice is to be made

OUTPUT — Gives the process results (Note:same as INPUT box)

FLOWLINE — Connects symbols and shows direction

CONNECTOR — Continues a chart to another point on the same page

OFF-PAGE CONNECTOR — Continues a chart to another page

4

POINTS TO REMEMBER:

An <u>OVAL</u> means the beginning and end of a flowchart; it indicates the terminal points. If you trace it, you will see that one "flowline leads out from START and into STOP.

A <u>PARALLELOGRAM</u> has two purposes, to show input and to show output. Input is information given to the computer. Information gotten from the computer is called output and is also put into a parallelogram. A parallelogram should have one line leading in and one line leading out.

A <u>RECTANGLE</u> represents work done. One task is presented in each box. It will always have one flowline leading in and one leading out.

A <u>DIAMOND</u> represents a decision. It is always phrased as a question which can be answered yes or no. A diamond will have one flowline leading in and two leading out, one marked YES and one marked NO.

A <u>LINE</u> with arrows indicates the direction of the flowchart. These <u>FLOWLINES</u> are always vertical or horizontal and meet each other at right angles. They must <u>never</u> cross each other.

A <u>CIRCLE</u> is used when the flowchart does not fit in the space. One circle has a number which corresponds to another circle on the sane page.

A <u>PENTAGON</u> means that a flowchart will be continued on the next page. The number put in the first pentagon matches the number in a second pentagon found on the following page.

NOTE: Flowcharts should follow a top-to-bottom and left-to-right progression a's much as possible.

Once the job is yours, a flowchart such as the one below may be used to determine what your weekly paycheck is.

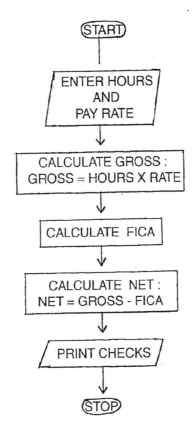

This is a very simple program flowchart, but may be all that is necessary to show the basic procedure. Note the two parallelograms and how their messages differ from those of the rectangles. A programmer might then take this and expand it to show other things — how FICA is determined, for example. You might want to try this if you know the formula for calculating FICA.

Below you will see three flowcharts which are used to solve math problems. The first is an incomplete chart for finding the average of five numbers. The second computes the batting average (B) of a baseball player, given his at-bats (A) and his hits (H). The third determines whether a given number is positive or negative. Complete each by enclosing the steps with the correct symbols and connecting with arrows. Since page 7 gives you the answers, you might want to fold the booklet over or cover the page as you are working to keep from looking at it.

6

#1	#2	#3
START	START	START
ENTER 29,467, 53,902,84	ENTER H, A	AENTER X=50,Y=30
8=29+467+53+ 902+84	B=H/A	D=X-Y
		YES
A=S/5	PRINT B	D>0?
		NO
PRINT A	STOP	PRINT NEGATIVE NUMBER
STOP		PRINT POSITIVE NUMBER
		STOP

Did your charts look like this?If so, great!If not, review pages 3-4. You may be wondering why there is an option to print negative number when the answer is obviously positive. Both options are needed in order to cover all variations of a problem. What if this were a *real* program and it had to handle a problem in which D = Y - X?Then the answer would have been 30-50, or -20.

7

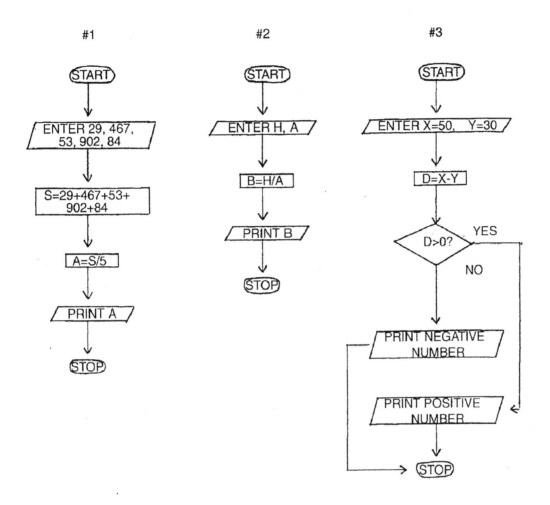

#1

START

ENTER 29, 467, 53, 902, 84

S=29+467+53+ 902+84

A=S/5

PRINT A

STOP

#2

START

ENTER H, A

B=H/A

PRINT B

STOP

#3

START

ENTER X=50, Y=30

D=X-Y

D>0?   YES

NO

PRINT NEGATIVE NUMBER

PRINT POSITIVE NUMBER

STOP

LOOPS:

A loop in a flowchart comes out of a decision box and enables you to return to an earlier point in the chart. To understand the use of the loop, let's look back at the flowchart for job-hunting which was on page 2. There are two loops represented by this flowchart.

The first came out of the diamond-shaped decision box reading *Get interview?* If the answer was *Yes,* you proceeded to make an appointment. If *No,* you *looped* back up to an earlier point and continued the job-hunt by submitting resume and application to another possible employer.

The second loop came from a *No* response to the decision box, *Is pay good?* When you decided *Yes,* the pay was good, you proceeded to accept the job. If you decided *No,* the pay was not good, you

8

returned to an earlier point, submitting your resume and application elsewhere. The flow-chart then guided you to repeat the same steps you had taken before. (NOTE:, Loops always flow from, decisions, symbolized in this guide by diamond-shaped boxes, and always return you to an earlier point. Understanding this simple process will help you trace through and understand the most complex flowchart.)

The flowchart that follows shows how to divide a number between 10 and 100 by a number that is less than 10. Study it and then answer the following:

1. This flowchart shows how many loops?

2. What decision is made first?

3. What should you do if the answer is *Yes?*

4. What should you do if the answer is *No?*

5. What is the second decision?

6. What should you do if the answer is *No?*

138

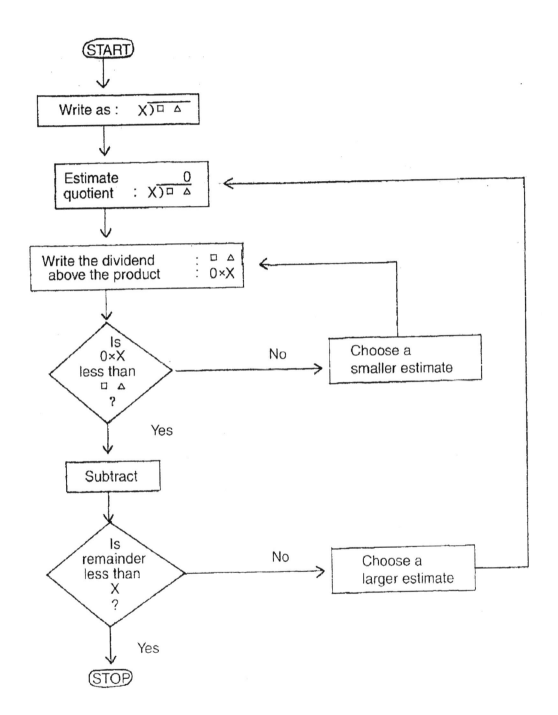

On the following page is an old, almost classic example of flowcharting, which has been titled *How to Get to Work in the Morning.* Use it to answer the questions that follow below. Answers to these questions can be found on the last page of this section.

7. Look at point (a) Does this represent a loop? Why or why not?

8. Bow many loops do you find in the chart? Do all the decision boxes in the chart produce loops? How can you tell?

9. What is the first decision? 10. If *Yes,* what do you do?

11. Look at the box that contains (b). Could that box read *How cold?* Why or why not?

12. Which step comes next if the answer at point (c) is *No?*

13. If the answer to the step at point (d) is *Yes,* what happens?

14. How many times does someone who is married more than 5 years get kissed?

15. How many times does a newlywed get kissed?

16. If point (d) had to be located on another page because of space limitations, what should (A) be changed to?

11

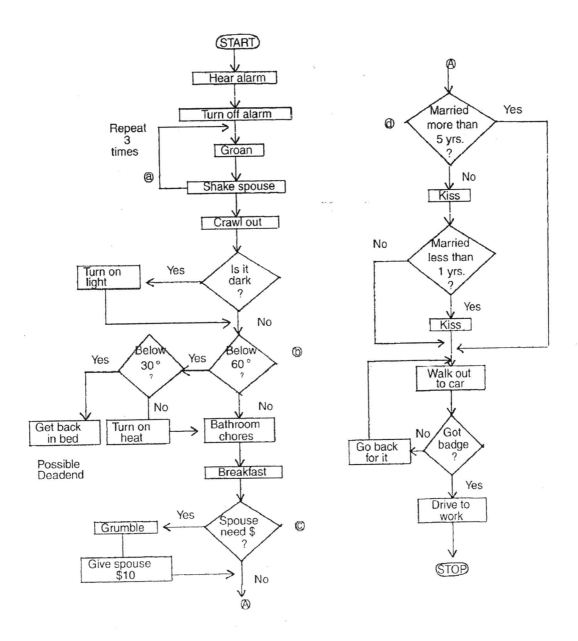

START

Hear alarm

Turn off alarm

Repeat 3 times

Groan

ⓐ

Shake spouse

Crawl out

Turn on light — Yes — Is it dark ?

No

Below 30° ? — Yes — Below 60° ? ⓑ

Yes

No

No

Get back in bed — Turn on heat → Bathroom chores

Possible Deadend

Breakfast

Grumble ← Yes — Spouse need $? ⓒ

Give spouse $10 → No

Ⓐ

Ⓐ

Married more than 5 yrs. ? ⓓ — Yes

No

Kiss

Married less than 1 yrs. ? — No

Yes

Kiss

Walk out to car

Go back for it ← No — Got badge ?

Yes

Drive to work

STOP

CANDY MACHINE FLOWCHART

START

MONEY INSERTED

6 NICKELS ?

4 NICKELS 1 DIME ?

2 NICKELS 2 DIMES ?

3 DIMES ?

QUARTER & NICKEL ?

QUARTER & DIME ?

2 QUARTERS ?

No / YES (repeated at each decision diamond)

RETURN 5¢

RETURN 15¢

SHOW "MAKE SELECTION"

Ⓐ Ⓑ Ⓒ Ⓓ ① ②

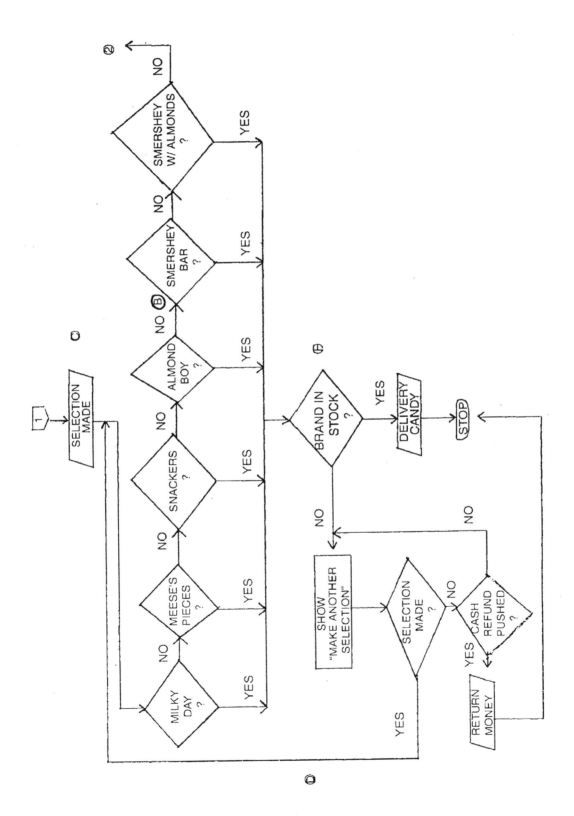

Please study the flowchart for a candy vending machine, then answer the following questions. The answers are at the end of the section.

17. How many brands of candy are available?

18. What is the price of each?

19. What coins may be used?

20. At point Ⓐ, what is the next function?

21. At point Ⓑ what is the next function?

22. Why is point Ⓒ a parallelogram?

23. What three steps immediately preceded point Ⓓ ?

24. If one were to reach point Ⓗ what would that MOST likely mean?

25. What might we call point Ⓓ?

26. At point Ⓔ what brands have been eliminated as selection options?

27. At point Ⓔ, what brands are still selection options?

28. Why is the box at Ⓕ a diamond shape?

29. What does a *Yes* decision at Ⓕ lead to?

30. Name two indicated input points.

31. Name two output boxes.

15

KEY (CORRECT ANSWERS)

ANSWERSTO QUESTIONS1-6.

1. Two.

2. Is OxX (the product) less than ?? (the dividend)?

3. Subtract the product from the dividend.

4. *Choose a smaller estimate* and go back to *Write the dividend ?? above the product* OxK to then see if the product is less than the dividend. In other words, you repeat the steps as the loop indicates.

5. *Is the remainder less than* X *(the divisor)?*

6. *Choose a larger estimate* and loop back to repeat the steps as the arrows indicate. You go all the way back to the rectangle immediately preceding the first decision box.

NOTE: Now look back at the flowchart again. See that the lines forming the loops never intersect (cross) each other.

ANSWERS TO *HOW TO GET TO WORK IN THE MORNING*

7. No, point ⓐ doesn't represent a loop. You know this because it doesn't flow from a decision box, a diamond-shaped box that requires a *Yes* or *No* answer.

8. There is only one loop in the chart. No, all the decision boxes in the chart don't produce loops. Only once does it come from a decision box <u>and</u> direct you <u>back</u> to repeat steps.This is at *Got badge?* Remember, loops refer you back to an earlier part in the chart. The only other item that looks like a loop is from *Shake spouse.* It's not a loop, however, it's a way of telling you to repeat an action without taking up space.

9. *Is it dark?* is the first decision.

10. If the answer is *Yes,* then you should *Turn on light.*

11. No, because decision boxes must be able to be answered *Yes* or *No* <u>only</u>.

12. The next step is point ⓓ, *Married more than 5 years?*

13. If the answer to the step at point ⓓ your car. is *Yes,* you walk out to

14. Someone who is married more than 5 years doesn't get kissed at all.

145

15. A newlywed gets kissed twice.

16. Under these circumstances, Ⓐ should be changed to ⟨ A ⟩; it would become an *off-page connector*.

ANSWERS TO THE *CANDY MACHINE FLOWCHART*

17. 6

18. 30 cents

19. Quarters, nickels and dimes

20. Show *make selection*

21. *Return 15¢*

22. It's a parallelogram because that shape signals input. We are assuming that a candy machine is a computer. In that case, the *keyboard* is the knobs or buttons that are pushed to make a selection or to get a refund. The *keyboard operator* is any person who comes to buy candy. He/she *enters* the data (the selection or the money), and so this is considered input.

23. (1) The selection made was not in stock.
    (2) The consumer was signaled to make another selection.
    (3) Another selection was made.

24. The *operator* did not put in enough money, he or she put in the wrong coins or wrong combination of coins, or the machine is out of order. By the time we get to point Ⓗ, all <u>likely</u>, possible combinations of the coins that will be taken have been exhausted. The flaw here is that there is no detailed provisio for occurrences like: putting in pennies, or putting in too much money. If the person were to put in three quarters, how would he or she get one back? This flowchart doesn't tell us, and this is a flaw in the algorithm.

25. A loop.

26. Milky Day, Meese's Pieces, Snackers, and Almond Boy.

27. Smershey Bar and Smershey with Almonds.

28. It is a decision box. It asks whether or not the brand is in stock.

29. *Deliver sandy*

30. Ⓖ and Ⓒ

31. *Deliver candy, Return 5¢, Return 15¢,* and/or *Return money*

GLOSSARY OF COMPUTER TERMS

Contents

GLOSSARY OF COMPUTER TERMS

Basic

application & app
An application (often called "app" for short) is simply a program with a GUI. Note that it is different from an applet.

boot
Starting up an OS is booting it. If the computer is already running, it is more often called rebooting.

browser
A browser is a program used to browse the web. Some common browsers include Netscape, MSIE (Microsoft Internet Explorer), Safari, Lynx, Mosaic, Amaya, Arena, Chimera, Opera, Cyberdog, HotJava, etc.

bug
A bug is a mistake in the design of something, especially software. A really severe bug can cause something to crash.

chat
Chatting is like e-mail, only it is done instantaneously and can directly involve multiple people at once. While e-mail now relies on one more or less standard protocol, chatting still has a couple competing ones. Of particular note are IRC and Instant Messenger. One step beyond chatting is called MUDding.

click
To press a mouse button. When done twice in rapid succession, it is referred to as a double-click.

cursor
A point of attention on the computer screen, often marked with a flashing line or block. Text typed into the computer will usually appear at the cursor.

database
A database is a collection of data, typically organized to make common retrievals easy and efficient. Some common database programs include Oracle, Sybase, Postgres, Informix, Filemaker, Adabas, etc.

desktop
A desktop system is a computer designed to sit in one position on a desk somewhere and not move around. Most general purpose computers are desktop systems. Calling a system a desktop implies nothing about its platform. The fastest desktop system at any given time is typically either an Alpha or PowerPC based system, but the SPARC and PA-RISC based systems are also often in the running. Industrial strength desktops are typically called workstations.

directory
Also called "folder", a directory is a collection of files typically created for organizational purposes. Note that a directory is itself a file, so a directory can generally contain other directories. It differs in this way from a partition.

disk
A disk is a physical object used for storing data. It will not forget its data when it loses power. It is always used in conjunction with a disk drive. Some disks can be removed from their drives, some cannot. Generally it is possible to write new information to a disk in addition to reading data from it, but this is not always the case.

drive
A device for storing and/or retrieving data. Some drives (such as disk drives, zip drives, and tape drives) are typically capable of having new data written to them, but some others (like CD-ROMs or DVD-ROMs) are not. Some drives have random access (like disk drives, zip drives, CD-ROMs, and DVD-ROMs), while others only have sequential access (like tape drives).

e-book
The concept behind an e-book is that it should provide all the functionality of an ordinary book but in a manner that is (overall) less expensive and more environmentally friendly. The actual term e-book is somewhat confusingly used to refer to a variety of things: custom software to play e-book titles, dedicated hardware to play e-book titles, and the e-book titles themselves. Individual e-book titles can be free or commercial (but will always be less expensive than their printed counterparts) and have to be loaded into a player to be read. Players vary wildly in capability level. Basic ones allow simple reading and bookmarking; better ones include various features like hypertext, illustrations, audio, and even limited video. Other optional features allow the user to mark-up sections of text, leave notes, circle or diagram things, highlight passages, program or customize settings, and even use interactive fiction. There are many types of e-book; a couple popular ones include the Newton book and Palm DOC.

e-mail
E-mail is short for electronic mail. It allows for the transfer of information from one computer to another, provided that they are hooked up via some sort of network (often the Internet. E-mail works similarly to FAXing, but its contents typically get printed out on the other end only on demand, not immediately and automatically as with FAX. A machine receiving e-mail will also not reject other incoming mail messages as a busy FAX machine will; rather they will instead be queued up to be received after the current batch has been completed. E-mail is only seven-bit clean, meaning that you should not expect anything other than ASCII data to go through uncorrupted without prior conversion via something like uucode or bcode. Some mailers will do some conversion automatically, but unless you know your mailer is one of them, you may want to do the encoding manually.

file
A file is a unit of (usually named) information stored on a computer.

firmware
Sort of in-between hardware and software, firmware consists of modifiable programs embedded in hardware. Firmware updates should be treated with care since they can literally destroy the underlying hardare if done improperly. There are also cases where neglecting to apply a firmware update can destroy the underlying hardware, so user beware.

floppy
An extremely common type of removable disk. Floppies do not hold too much data, but most computers are capable of reading them. Note though that there are different competing format used for floppies, so that a floppy written by one type of computer might not directly work on another. Also sometimes called "diskette".

format
The manner in which data is stored; its organization. For example, VHS, SVHS, and Beta are three different formats of video tape. They are not 100% compatible with each other, but information can be transferred from one to the other with the proper equipment (but not always without loss; SVHS contains more information than either of the other two). Computer information can be stored in literally hundreds of different formats, and can represent text, sounds, graphics, animations, etc. Computer information can be exchanged via different computer types provided both computers can interpret the format used.

function keys
On a computer keyboard, the keys that start with an "F" that are usually (but not always) found on the top row. They are meant to perform user-defined tasks.

3

graphics
Anything visually displayed on a computer that is not text.

hardware
The physical portion of the computer.

hypertext
A hypertext document is like a text document with the ability to contain pointers to other regions of (possibly other) hypertext documents.

Internet
The Internet is the world-wide network of computers. There is only one Internet, and thus it is typically capitalized (although it is sometimes referred to as "the 'net"). It is different from an intranet.

keyboard
A keyboard on a computer is almost identical to a keyboard on a typewriter. Computer keyboards will typically have extra keys, however. Some of these keys (common examples include Control, Alt, and Meta) are meant to be used in conjunction with other keys just like shift on a regular typewriter. Other keys (common examples include Insert, Delete, Home, End, Help, function keys,etc.) are meant to be used independently and often perform editing tasks. Keyboards on different platforms will often look slightly different and have somewhat different collections of keys. Some keyboards even have independent shift lock and caps lock keys. Smaller keyboards with only math-related keys are typically called "keypads".

language
Computer programs can be written in a variety of different languages. Different languages are optimized for different tasks. Common languages include Java, C, C++, ForTran, Pascal, Lisp, and BASIC. Some people classify languages into two categories, higher-level and lower-level. These people would consider assembly language and machine language lower-level languages and all other languages higher-level. In general, higher-level languages can be either interpreted or compiled; many languages allow both, but some are restricted to one or the other. Many people do not consider machine language and assembly language at all when talking about programming languages.

laptop
A laptop is any computer designed to do pretty much anything a desktop system can do but run for a short time (usually two to five hours) on batteries. They are designed to be carried around but are not particularly convenient to carry around. They are significantly more expensive than desktop systems and have far worse battery life than PDAs. Calling a system a laptop implies nothing about its platform. By far the fastest laptops are the PowerPC based Macintoshes.

memory
Computer memory is used to temporarily store data. In reality, computer memory is only capable of remembering sequences of zeros and ones, but by utilizing the binary number system it is possible to produce arbitrary rational numbers and through clever formatting all manner of representations of pictures, sounds, and animations. The most common types of memory are RAM, ROM, and flash.

MHz & megahertz
One megahertz is equivalent to 1000 kilohertz, or 1,000,000 hertz. The clock speed of the main processor of many computers is measured in MHz, and is sometimes (quite misleadingly) used to represent the overall speed of a computer. In fact, a computer's speed is based upon many factors, and since MHz only reveals how many clock cycles the main processor has per second (saying nothing about how much is actually accomplished per cycle), it can really only accurately be used to gauge two computers with the same generation and family of processor plus similar configurations of memory, co-processors, and other peripheral hardware.

modem
A modem allows two computers to communicate over ordinary phone lines. It derives its name

from **mod**ulate / **dem**odulate, the process by which it converts digital computer data back and forth for use with an analog phone line.

monitor

The screen for viewing computer information is called a monitor.

mouse

In computer parlance a mouse can be both the physical object moved around to control a pointer on the screen, and the pointer itself. Unlike the animal, the proper plural of computer mouse is "mouses".

multimedia

This originally indicated a capability to work with and integrate various types of things including audio, still graphics, and especially video. Now it is more of a marketing term and has little real meaning. Historically the Amiga was the first multimedia machine. Today in addition to AmigaOS, IRIX and Solaris are popular choices for high-end multimedia work.

NC

The term **network computer** refers to any (usually desktop) computer system that is designed to work as part of a network rather than as a stand-alone machine. This saves money on hardware, software, and maintenance by taking advantage of facilities already available on the network. The term "Internet appliance" is often used interchangeably with NC.

network

A network (as applied to computers) typically means a group of computers working together. It can also refer to the physical wire etc. connecting the computers.

notebook

A notebook is a small laptop with similar price, performance, and battery life.

organizer

An organizer is a tiny computer used primarily to store names, addresses, phone numbers, and date book information. They usually have some ability to exchange information with desktop systems. They boast even better battery life than PDAs but are far less capable. They are extremely inexpensive but are typically incapable of running any special purpose applications and are thus of limited use.

OS

The **operating system** is the program that manages a computer's resources. Common OSes include Windows '95, MacOS, Linux, Solaris, AmigaOS, AIX, Windows NT, etc.

PC

The term **personal computer** properly refers to any desktop, laptop, or notebook computer system. Its use is inconsistent, though, and some use it to specifically refer to x86 based systems running MS-DOS, MS-Windows, GEOS, or OS/2. This latter use is similar to what is meant by a WinTel system.

PDA

A **personal digital assistant** is a small battery-powered computer intended to be carried around by the user rather than left on a desk. This means that the processor used ought to be power-efficient as well as fast, and the OS ought to be optimized for hand-held use. PDAs typically have an instant-on feature (they would be useless without it) and most are grayscale rather than color because of battery life issues. Most have a pen interface and come with a detachable stylus. None use mouses. All have some ability to exchange data with desktop systems. In terms of raw capabilities, a PDA is more capable than an organizer and less capable than a laptop (although some high-end PDAs beat out some low-end laptops). By far the most popular PDA is the Pilot, but other common types include Newtons, Psions, Zauri, Zoomers, and Windows CE hand-helds. By far the fastest current PDA is the Newton (based around a StrongARM RISC processor). Other PDAs are optimized for other tasks; few computers are as personal as PDAs and care must be taken in their purchase. Feneric's PDA / Handheld Comparison Page is perhaps the most detailed comparison of PDAs and handheld computers to be found anywhere on the web.

platform
Roughly speaking, a platform represents a computer's family. It is defined by both the processor type on the hardware side and the OS type on the software side. Computers belonging to different platforms cannot typically run each other's programs (unless the programs are written in a language like Java).

portable
If something is portable it can be easily moved from one type of computer to another. The verb "to port" indicates the moving itself.

printer
A printer is a piece of hardware that will print computer information onto paper.

processor
The processor (also called central processing unit, or CPU) is the part of the computer that actually works with the data and runs the programs. There are two main processor types in common usage today: CISC and RISC. Some computers have more than one processor and are thus called "multiprocessor". This is distinct from multitasking. Advertisers often use megahertz numbers as a means of showing a processor's speed. This is often extremely misleading; megahertz numbers are more or less meaningless when compared across different types of processors.

program
A program is a series of instructions for a computer, telling it what to do or how to behave. The terms "application" and "app" mean almost the same thing (albeit applications generally have GUIs). It is however different from an applet. Program is also the verb that means to create a program, and a programmer is one who programs.

run
Running a program is how it is made to do something. The term "execute" means the same thing.

software
The non-physical portion of the computer; the part that exists only as data; the programs. Another term meaning much the same is "code".

spreadsheet
An program used to perform various calculations. It is especially popular for financial applications. Some common spreadsheets include Lotus 123, Excel, OpenOffice Spreadsheet, Octave, Gnumeric, AppleWorks Spreadsheet, Oleo, and GeoCalc.

user
The operator of a computer.

word processor
A program designed to help with the production of textual documents, like letters and memos. Heavier duty work can be done with a desktop publisher. Some common word processors include MS-Word, OpenOffice Write, WordPerfect, AbiWord, AppleWorks Write, and GeoWrite.

www
The World-Wide-Web refers more or less to all the publically accessable documents on the Internet. It is used quite loosely, and sometimes indicates only HTML files and sometimes FTP and Gopher files, too. It is also sometimes just referred to as "the web".

6

Reference

65xx

The 65xx series of processors includes the 6502, 65C02, 6510, 8502, 65C816, 65C816S, etc. It is a CISC design and is not being used in too many new stand-alone computer systems, but is still being used in embedded systems, game systems (such as the Super NES), and processor enhancement add-ons for older systems. It was originally designed by MOS Technologies, but is now produced by The Western Design Center, Inc. It was the primary processor for many extremely popular systems no longer being produced, including the Commodore 64, the Commodore 128, and all the Apple][series machines.

68xx

The 68xx series of processors includes the 6800, 6805, 6809, 68000, 68020, 68030, 68040, 68060, etc. It is a CISC design and is not being used in too many new stand-alone computer systems, but is still being used heavily in embedded systems. It was originally designed by Motorola and was the primary processor for older generations of many current machines, including Macintoshes, Amigas, Sun workstations, HP workstations, etc. and the primary processor for many systems no longer being produced, such as the TRS-80. The PowerPC was designed in part to be its replacement.

a11y

Commonly used to abbreviate the word "accessibility". There are eleven letters between the "a" and the "y".

ADA

An object-oriented language at one point popular for military and some academic software. Lately C++ and Java have been getting more attention.

AI

Artificial intelligence is the concept of making computers do tasks once considered to require thinking. AI makes computers play chess, recognize handwriting and speech, helps suggest prescriptions to doctors for patients based on imput symptoms, and many other tasks, both mundane and not.

AIX

The industrial strength OS designed by IBM to run on PowerPC and x86 based machines. It is a variant of UNIX and is meant to provide more power than OS/2.

AJaX

AJaX is a little like DHTML, but it adds asynchronous communication between the browser and Web site via either XML or JSON to achieve performance that often rivals desktop applications.

Alpha

An Alpha is a RISC processor invented by Digital and currently produced by Digital/Compaq and Samsung. A few different OSes run on Alpha based machines including Digital UNIX, Windows NT, Linux, NetBSD, and AmigaOS. Historically, at any given time, the fastest processor in the world has usually been either an Alpha or a PowerPC (with sometimes SPARCs and PA-RISCs making the list), but Compaq has recently announced that there will be no further development of this superb processor instead banking on the release of the somewhat suspect Merced.

AltiVec

AltiVec (also called the "Velocity Engine") is a special extension built into some PowerPC CPUs to provide better performance for certain operations, most notably graphics and sound. It is similar to MMX on the x86 CPUs. Like MMX, it requires special software for full performance benefits to be realized.

Amiga

A platform originally created and only produced by Commodore, but now owned by Gateway 2000 and produced by it and a few smaller companies. It was historically the first multimedia machine and gave the world of computing many innovations. It is now primarily used for audio / video applications; in fact, a decent Amiga system is less expensive than a less capable video editing system. Many music videos were created on Amigas, and a few television series and movies had their special effects generated on Amigas. Also, Amigas can be readily synchronized with video cameras, so typically when a computer screen appears on television or in a movie and it is not flickering wildly, it is probably an Amiga in disguise. Furthermore, many coin-operated arcade games are really Amigas packaged in stand-up boxes. Amigas have AmigaOS for their OS. New Amigas have either a PowerPC or an Alpha for their main processor and a 68xx processor dedicated to graphics manipulation. Older (and low end) Amigas do everything with just a 68xx processor.

AmigaOS
The OS used by Amigas. AmigaOS combines the functionality of an OS and a window manager and is fully multitasking. AmigaOS boasts a pretty good selection of games (many arcade games are in fact written on Amigas) but has limited driver support. AmigaOS will run on 68xx, Alpha, and PowerPC based machines.

Apple][
The Apple][computer sold millions of units and is generally considered to have been the first home computer with a 1977 release date. It is based on the 65xx family of processors. The earlier Apple I was only available as a build-it-yourself kit.

AppleScript
A scripting language for Mac OS computers.

applet
An applet differs from an application in that is not meant to be run stand-alone but rather with the assistance of another program, usually a browser.

AppleTalk
AppleTalk is a protocol for computer networks. It is arguably inferior to TCP/IP.

Aqua
The default window manager for Mac OS X.

Archie
Archie is a system for searching through FTP archives for particular files. It tends not to be used too much anymore as more general modern search engines are significantly more capable.

ARM
An ARM is a RISC processor invented by Advanced RISC Machines, currently owned by Intel, and currently produced by both the above and Digital/Compaq. ARMs are different from most other processors in that they were not designed to maximize speed but rather to maximize speed per power consumed. Thus ARMs find most of their use on hand-held machines and PDAs. A few different OSes run on ARM based machines including Newton OS, JavaOS, and (soon) Windows CE and Linux. The StrongARM is a more recent design of the original ARM, and it is both faster and more power efficient than the original.

ASCII
The ASCII character set is the most popular one in common use. People will often refer to a bare text file without complicated embedded format instructions as an ASCII file, and such files can usually be transferred from one computer system to another with relative ease. Unfortunately there are a few minor variations of it that pop up here and there, and if you receive a text file that seems subtly messed up with punctuation marks altered or upper and lower case reversed, you are probably encountering one of the ASCII variants. It is usually fairly straightforward to translate from one ASCII variant to another, though. The ASCII character set is seven bit while pure binary is usually eight bit, so transferring a binary file through ASCII channels will result in corruption and loss of data. Note also that the ASCII character set is a

subset of the Unicode character set.

ASK

A protocol for an infrared communications port on a device. It predates the IrDA compliant infrared communications protocol and is not compatible with it. Many devices with infrared communications support both, but some only support one or the other.

assembly language

Assembly language is essentially machine language that has had some of the numbers replaced by somewhat easier to remember mnemonics in an attempt to make it more human-readable. The program that converts assembly language to machine language is called an assembler. While assembly language predates FORTRAN, it is not typically what people think of when they discuss computer languages.

Atom

Atom is an intended replacement for RSS and like it is used for syndicating a web site's content. It is currently not nearly as popular or well-supported by software applications, however.

authoring system

Any GUIs method of designing new software can be called an authoring system. Any computer language name with the word "visual" in front of it is probably a version of that language built with some authoring system capabilities. It appears that the first serious effort to produce a commercial quality authoring system took place in the mid eighties for the Amiga.

AWK

AWK is an interpreted language developed in 1977 by Aho, Weinberger, & Kernighan. It gets its name from its creators' initials. It is not particularly fast, but it was designed for creating small throwaway programs rather than full-blown applications -- it is designed to make the writing of the program fast, not the program itself. It is quite portable with versions existing for numerous platforms, including a free GNU version. Plus, virtually every version of UNIX in the world comes with AWK built-in.

BASIC

The **B**eginners' **A**ll-purpose **S**ymbolic **I**nstruction **C**ode is a computer language developed by Kemeny & Kurtz in 1964. Although it is traditionally interpreted, compilers exist for many platforms. While the interpreted form is typically fairly slow, the compiled form is often quite fast, usually faster than Pascal. The biggest problem with BASIC is portability; versions for different machines are often completely unlike each other; Amiga BASIC at first glance looks more like Pascal, for example. Portability problems actually go beyond even the cross platform level; in fact, most machines have multiple versions of incompatible BASICs available for use. The most popular version of BASIC today is called Visual BASIC. Like all BASICs it has portability issues, but it has some of the advantages of an authoring system so it is relatively easy to use.

baud

A measure of communications speed, used typically for modems indicating how many bits per second can be transmitted.

BBS

A **b**ulletin **b**oard **s**ystem is a computer that can be directly connected to via modem and provides various services like e-mail, chatting, newsgroups, and file downloading. BBSs have waned in popularity as more and more people are instead connecting to the Internet, but they are still used for product support and local area access. Most current BBSs provide some sort of gateway connection to the Internet.

bcode

Identical in intent to uucode, bcode is slightly more efficient and more portable across different computer types. It is the preferred method used by MIME.

BeOS

A lightweight OS available for both PowerPC and x86 based machines. It is often referred to simply as "Be".

beta
A beta version of something is not yet ready for prime time but still possibly useful to related developers and other interested parties. Expect beta software to crash more than properly released software does. Traditionally beta versions (of commercial software) are distributed only to selected testers who are often then given a discount on the proper version after its release in exchange for their testing work. Beta versions of non-commercial software are more often freely available to anyone who has an interest.

binary
There are two meanings for binary in common computer usage. The first is the name of the number system in which there are only zeros and ones. This is important to computers because all computer data is ultimately a series of zeros and ones, and thus can be represented by binary numbers. The second is an offshoot of the first; data that is not meant to be intepreted through a common character set (like ASCII) is typically referred to as binary data. Pure binary data is typically eight bit data, and transferring a binary file through ASCII channels without prior modification will result in corruption and loss of data. Binary data can be turned into ASCII data via uucoding or bcoding.

bit
A bit can either be on or off; one or zero. All computer data can ultimately be reduced to a series of bits. The term is also used as a (very rough) measure of sound quality, color quality, and even procesor capability by considering the fact that series of bits can represent binary numbers. For example (without getting too technical), an eight bit image can contain at most 256 distinct colors while a sixteen bit image can contain at most 65,536 distinct colors.

bitmap
A bitmap is a simplistic representation of an image on a computer, simply indicating whether or not pixels are on or off, and sometimes indicating their color. Often fonts are represented as bitmaps. The term "pixmap" is sometimes used similarly; typically when a distinction is made, pixmap refers to color images and bitmap refers to monochrome images.

blog
Short for web log, a blog (or weblog, or less commonly, 'blog) is a web site containing periodic (usually frequent) posts. Blogs are usually syndicated via either some type of RSS or Atom and often supports TrackBacks. It is not uncommon for blogs to function much like newspaper columns. A blogger is someone who writes for and maintains a blog.

boolean
Boolean algebra is the mathematics of base two numbers. Since base two numbers have only two values, zero and one, there is a good analogy between base two numbers and the logical values "true" & "false". In common usage, booleans are therefore considered to be simple logical values like true & false and the operations that relate them, most typically "and", "or" and "not". Since everyone has a basic understanding of the concepts of true & false and basic conjunctions, everyone also has a basic understanding of boolean concepts -- they just may not realize it.

byte
A byte is a grouping of bits. It is typically eight bits, but there are those who use non-standard byte sizes. Bytes are usually measured in large groups, and the term "kilobyte" (often abbreviated as K) means one-thousand twenty-four (1024) bytes; the term "megabyte" (often abbreviated as M) means one-thousand twenty-four (1024) K; the term gigabyte (often abbreviated as G) means one-thousand twenty-four (1024) M; and the term "terabyte" (often abbreviated as T) means one-thousand twenty-four (1024) G. Memory is typically measured in kilobytes or megabytes, and disk space is typically measured in megabytes or gigabytes. Note that the multipliers here are 1024 instead of the more common 1000 as would be used in the metric system. This is to make it easier to work with the binary number system. Note also that some hardware manufacturers will use the smaller 1000 multiplier on M & G quantities to make

their disk drives seem larger than they really are; buyer beware.

bytecode

Sometimes computer languages that are said to be either interpreted or compiled are in fact neither and are more accurately said to be somewhere in between. Such languages are compiled into bytecode which is then interpreted on the target system. Bytecode tends to be binary but will work on any machine with the appropriate runtime environment (or virtual machine) for it.

C

C is one of the most popular computer languages in the world, and quite possibly *the* most popular. It is a compiled langauge widely supported on many platforms. It tends to be more portable than FORTRAN but less portable than Java; it has been standardized by ANSI as "ANSI C" -- older versions are called either "K&R C" or "Kernighan and Ritchie C" (in honor of C's creators), or sometimes just "classic C". Fast and simple, it can be applied to all manner of general purpose tasks. C compilers are made by several companies, but the free GNU version (gcc) is still considered one of the best. Newer C-like object-oriented languages include both Java and C++.

C#

C# is a compiled object-oriented language based heavily on C++ with some Java features.

C++

C++ is a compiled object-oriented language. Based heavily on C, C++ is nearly as fast and can often be thought of as being just C with added features. It is currently probably the second most popular object-oriented language, but it has the drawback of being fairly complex -- the much simpler but somewhat slower Java is probably the most popular object-oriented language. Note that C++ was developed independently of the somewhat similar Objective-C; it is however related to Objective-C++.

C64/128

The Commodore 64 computer to this day holds the record for being the most successful model of computer ever made with even the lowest estimates being in the tens of millions. Its big brother, the Commodore 128, was not quite as popular but still sold several million units. Both units sported ROM-based BASIC and used it as a default "OS". The C128 also came with CP/M (it was a not-often-exercized option on the C64). In their later days they were also packaged with GEOS. Both are based on 65xx family processors. They are still in use today and boast a friendly and surprisingly active user community. There is even a current effort to port Linux to the C64 and C128 machines.

CDE

The **c**ommon **d**esktop **e**nvironment is a popular commercial window manager (and much more -- as its name touts, it is more of a desktop environment) that runs under X-Windows. Free work-alike versions are also available.

chain

Some computer devices support chaining, the ability to string multiple devices in a sequence plugged into just one computer port. Often, but not always, such a chain will require some sort of terminator to mark the end. For an example, a SCSI scanner may be plugged into a SCSI CD-ROM drive that is plugged into a SCSI hard drive that is in turn plugged into the main computer. For all these components to work properly, the scanner would also have to have a proper terminator in use. Device chaining has been around a long time, and it is interesting to note that C64/128 serial devices supported it from the very beginning. Today the most common low-cost chainable devices in use support USB while the fastest low-cost chainable devices in use support FireWire.

character set

Since in reality all a computer can store are series of zeros and ones, representing common things like text takes a little work. The solution is to view the series of zeros and ones instead as a sequence of bytes, and map each one to a particular letter, number, or symbol. The full mapping is called a character set. The most popular character set is commonly referred to as ASCII. The second most popular character set these days is Unicode (and it will probably eventually surpass ASCII). Other fairly common character sets include EBCDIC and PETSCII. They are generally quite different from one another; programs exist to convert between them on most platforms, though. Usually EBCDIC is only found on really old machines.

CISC
Complex instruction set computing is one of the two main types of processor design in use today. It is slowly losing popularity to RISC designs; currently all the fastest processors in the world are RISC. The most popular current CISC processor is the x86, but there are also still some 68xx, 65xx, and Z80s in use.

CLI
A command-line interface is a text-based means of communicating with a program, especially an OS. This is the sort of interface used by MS-DOS, or a UNIX shell window.

COBOL
The Common Business Oriented Language is a language developed back in 1959 and still used by some businesses. While it is relatively portable, it is still disliked by many professional programmers simply because COBOL programs tend to be physically longer than equivalent programs written in almost any other language in common use.

compiled
If a program is compiled, its original human-readable source has been converted into a form more easily used by a computer prior to it being run. Such programs will generally run more quickly than interpreted programs, because time was pre-spent in the compilation phase. A program that compiles other programs is called a compiler.

compression
It is often possible to remove redundant information or capitalize on patterns in data to make a file smaller. Usually when a file has been compressed, it cannot be used until it is uncompressed. Image files are common exceptions, though, as many popular image file formats have compression built-in.

cookie
A cookie is a small file that a web page on another machine writes to your personal machine's disk to store various bits of information. Many people strongly detest cookies and the whole idea of them, and most browsers allow the reception of cookies to be disabled or at least selectively disabled, but it should be noted that both Netscape and MSIE have silent cookie reception enabled by default. Sites that maintain shopping carts or remember a reader's last position have legitimate uses for cookies. Sites without such functionality that still spew cookies with distant (or worse, non-existent) expiration dates should perhaps be treated with a little caution.

CP/M
An early DOS for desktops, CP/M runs on both Z80 and the x86 based machines. CP/M provides only a CLI and there really is not any standard way to get a window manager to run on top of it. It is fairly complex and tricky to use. In spite of all this, CP/M was once the most popular DOS and is still in use today.

crash
If a bug in a program is severe enough, it can cause that program to crash, or to become inoperable without being restarted. On machines that are not multitasking, the entire machine will crash and have to be rebooted. On machines that are only partially multitasking the entire machine will sometimes crash and have to be rebooted. On machines that are fully multitasking, the machine should never crash and require a reboot.

Cray
A Cray is a high-end computer used for research and frequently heavy-duty graphics applications. Modern Crays typically have Solaris for their OS and sport sixty-four RISC

processors; older ones had various other configurations. Current top-of-the-line Crays can have over 2000 processors.

crippleware

Crippleware is a variant of shareware that will either self-destruct after its trial period or has built-in limitations to its functionality that get removed after its purchase.

CSS

Cascading style sheets are used in conjunction with HTML and XHTML to define the layout of web pages. While CSS is how current web pages declare how they should be displayed, it tends not to be supported well (if at all) by ancient browsers. XSL performs this same function more generally.

desktop publisher

A program for creating newspapers, magazines, books, etc. Some common desktop publishing programs include FrameMaker, PageMaker, InDesign, and GeoPublish.

DHTML

Dynamic HTML is simply the combined use of both CSS and JavaScript together in the same document; a more extreme form is called AJaX. Note that DHTML is quite different from the similarly named DTML.

dict

A protocol used for looking up definitions across a network (in particular the Internet).

digital camera

A digital camera looks and behaves like a regular camera, except instead of using film, it stores the image it sees in memory as a file for later transfer to a computer. Many digital cameras offer additional storage besides their own internal memory; a few sport some sort of disk but the majority utilize some sort of flash card. Digital cameras currently lack the resolution and color palette of real cameras, but are usually much more convenient for computer applications. Another related device is called a scanner.

DIMM

A physical component used to add RAM to a computer. Similar to, but incompatible with, SIMMs.

DNS

Domain name service is the means by which a name (like www.saugus.net or ftp.saugus.net) gets converted into a real Internet address that points to a particular machine.

DoS

In a denial of service attack, many individual (usually compromised) computers are used to try and simultaneously access the same public resource with the intent of overburdening it so that it will not be able to adequately serve its normal users.

DOS

A disk operating system manages disks and other system resources. Sort of a subset of OSes, sort of an archaic term for the same. MS-DOS is the most popular program currently calling itself a DOS. CP/M was the most popular prior to MS-DOS.

download

To download a file is to copy it from a remote computer to your own. The opposite is upload.

DR-DOS

The DOS currently produced by Caldera (originally produced by Design Research as a successor to CP/M) designed to work like MS-DOS. While similar to CP/M in many ways, it utilizes simpler commands. It provides only a CLI, but either Windows 3.1 or GEOS may be run on top of it to provide a GUI. It only runs on x86 based machines.

driver

A driver is a piece of software that works with the OS to control a particular piece of hardware, like a printer or a scanner or a mouse or whatever.

DRM

Depending upon whom you ask, DRM can stand for either Digital Rights Management or Digital Restrictions Management. In either case, DRM is used to place restrictions upon the usage of digital media ranging from software to music to video.

DTML

The **D**ocument **T**emplate **M**ark-up **L**anguage is a subset of SGML and a superset of HTML used for creating documents that dynamically adapt to external conditions using its own custom tags and a little bit of Python. Note that it is quite different from the similarly named DHTML.

EDBIC

The EDBIC character set is similar to (but less popular than) the ASCII character set in concept, but is significantly different in layout. It tends to be found only on old machines..

emacs

Emacs is both one of the most powerful and one of the most popular text editing programs in existence. Versions can be found for most platforms, and in fact multiple companies make versions, so for a given platform there might even be a choice. There is even a free GNU version available. The drawback with emacs is that it is not in the least bit lightweight. In fact, it goes so far in the other direction that even its advocates will occasionally joke about it. It is however extremely capable. Almost anything that one would need to relating to text can be done with emacs and is probably built-in. Even if one manages to find something that emacs was not built to do, emacs has a built-in Lisp interpreter capable of not only extending its text editing capabilities, but even of being used as a scripting language in its own right.

embedded

An embedded system is a computer that lives inside another device and acts as a component of that device. For example, current cars have an embedded computer under the hood that helps regulate much of their day to day operation.

An embedded file is a file that lives inside another and acts as a portion of that file. This is frequently seen with HTML files having embedded audio files; audio files often embedded in HTML include AU files, MIDI files, SID files, WAV files, AIFF files, and MOD files. Most browsers will ignore these files unless an appropriate plug-in is present.

emulator

An emulator is a program that allows one computer platform to mimic another for the purposes of running its software. Typically (but not always) running a program through an emulator will not be quite as pleasant an experience as running it on the real system.

endian

A processor will be either "big endian" or "little endian" based upon the manner in which it encodes multiple byte values. There is no difference in performance between the two encoding methods, but it is one of the sources of difficulty when reading binary data on different platforms.

environment

An environment (sometimes also called a runtime environment) is a collection of external variable items or parameters that a program can access when run. Information about the computer's hardware and the user can often be found in the environment.

EPOC

EPOC is a lightweight OS. It is most commonly found on the Psion PDA.

extension

Filename extensions originate back in the days of CP/M and basically allow a very rough grouping of different file types by putting a tag at the end of the name. To further complicate matters, the tag is sometimes separated by the name proper by a period "." and sometimes by a tab. While extensions are semi-enforced on CP/M, MS-DOS, and MS-Windows, they have no real meaning aside from convention on other platforms and are only optional.

FAQ

A **f**requently **a**sked **q**uestions file attempts to provide answers for all commonly asked questions

related to a given topic.
FireWire
An incredibly fast type of serial port that offers many of the best features of SCSI at a lower price. Faster than most types of parallel port, a single FireWire port is capable of chaining many devices without the need of a terminator. FireWire is similar in many respects to USB but is significantly faster and somewhat more expensive. It is heavily used for connecting audio/video devices to computers, but is also used for connecting storage devices like drives and other assorted devices like printers and scanners.
fixed width
As applied to a font, fixed width means that every character takes up the same amount of space. That is, an "i" will be just as wide as an "m" with empty space being used for padding. The opposite is variable width. The most common fixed width font is Courier.
flash
Flash memory is similar to RAM. It has one significant advantage: it does not lose its contents when power is lost; it has two main disadvantages: it is slower, and it eventually wears out. Flash memory is frequently found in PCMCIA cards.
font
In a simplistic sense, a font can be thought of as the physical description of a character set. While the character set will define what sets of bits map to what letters, numbers, and other symbols, the font will define what each letter, number, and other symbol looks like. Fonts can be either fixed width or variable width and independently, either bitmapped or vectored. The size of the large characters in a font is typically measured in points.
Forth
A language developed in 1970 by Moore. Forth is fairly portable and has versions on many different platforms. While it is no longer an very popular language, many of its ideas and concepts have been carried into other computer programs. In particular, some programs for doing heavy-duty mathematical and engineering work use Forth-like interfaces.
FORTRAN
FORTRAN stands for **formula translation** and is the oldest computer language in the world. It is typically compiled and is quite fast. Its primary drawbacks are portability and ease-of-use -- often different FORTRAN compilers on different platforms behave quite differently in spite of standardization efforts in 1966 (FORTRAN 66 or FORTRAN IV), 1978 (FORTRAN 77), and 1991 (FORTRAN 90). Today languages like C and Java are more popular, but FORTRAN is still heavily used in military software. It is somewhat amusing to note that when FORTRAN was first released back in 1958 its advocates thought that it would mean the end of software bugs. In truth of course by making the creation of more complex software practical, computer languages have merely created new types of software bugs.
FreeBSD
A free variant of Berkeley UNIX available for Alpha and x86 based machines. It is not as popular as Linux.
freeware
Freeware is software that is available for free with no strings attached. The quality is often superb as the authors are also generally users.
FTP
The **file transfer protocol** is one of the most commonly used methods of copying files across the Internet. It has its origins on UNIX machines, but has been adapted to almost every type of computer in existence and is built into many browsers. Most FTP programs have two modes of operation, ASCII, and binary. Transmitting an ASCII file via the ASCII mode of operation is more efficient and cleaner. Transmitting a binary file via the ASCII mode of operation will result in a broken binary file. Thus the FTP programs that do not support both modes of operation will typically only do the binary mode, as binary transfers are capable of transferring both kinds of

data without corruption.

gateway
A gateway connects otherwise separate computer networks.

GEOS
The **g**raphic **e**nvironment **o**perating **s**ystem is a lightweight OS with a GUI. It runs on several different processors, including the 65xx (different versions for different machines -- there are versions for the C64, the C128, and the Apple][, each utilizing the relevant custom chip sets), the x86 (although the x86 version is made to run on top of MS-DOS (or PC-DOS or DR-DOS) and is not strictly a full OS or a window manager, rather it is somewhat in between, like Windows 3.1) and numerous different PDAs, embedded devices, and hand-held machines. It was originally designed by Berkeley Softworks (no real relation to the Berkeley of UNIX fame) but is currently in a more interesting state: the company GeoWorks develops and promotes development of GEOS for hand-held devices, PDAs, & and embedded devices and owns (but has ceased further development on) the x86 version. The other versions are owned (and possibly still being developed) by the company CMD.

GHz & gigahertz
One gigahertz is equivalent to 1000 megahertz, or 1,000,000,000 hertz.

Glulx
A virtual machine optimized for running interactive fiction, interactive tutorials, and other interactive things of a primarily textual nature. Glulx has been ported to several platforms, and in in many ways an upgrade to the Z-machine.

GNOME
The **G**NU **n**etwork **o**bject **m**odel **e**nvironment is a popular free window manager (and much more -- as its name touts, it is more of a desktop environment) that runs under X-Windows. It is a part of the GNU project.

GNU
GNU stands for GNU's not UNIX and is thus a recursive acronym (and unlike the animal name, the "G" here is pronounced). At any rate, the GNU project is an effort by the Free Software Foundation (FSF) to make all of the traditional UNIX utilities free for whoever wants them. The Free Software Foundation programmers know their stuff, and the quality of the GNU software is on par with the best produced commercially, and often better. All of the GNU software can be downloaded for free or obtained on CD-ROM for a small service fee. Documentation for all GNU software can be downloaded for free or obtained in book form for a small service fee. The Free Software Foundation pays its bills from the collection of service fees and the sale of T-shirts, and exists mostly through volunteer effort. It is based in Cambridge, MA.

gopher
Though not as popular as FTP or http, the gopher protocol is implemented by many browsers and numerous other programs and allows the transfer of files across networks. In some respects it can be thought of as a hybrid between FTP and http, although it tends not to be as good at raw file transfer as FTP and is not as flexible as http. The collection of documents available through gopher is often called "gopherspace", and it should be noted that gopherspace is older than the web. It should also be noted that gopher is not getting as much attention as it once did, and surfing through gopherspace is a little like exploring a ghost town, but there is an interesting VR interface available for it, and some things in gopherspace still have not been copied onto the web.

GUI
A **g**raphical **u**ser **i**nterface is a graphics-based means of communicating with a program, especially an OS or window manager. In fact, a window manager can be thought of as a GUI for a CLI OS.

HP-UX
HP-UX is the version of UNIX designed by Hewlett-Packard to work with their PA-RISC and

68xx based machines.

HTML

The **H**ypertext **M**ark-up **L**anguage is the language currently most frequently used to express web pages (although it is rapidly being replaced by XHTML). Every browser has the built-in ability to understand HTML. Some browsers can additionally understand Java and browse FTP areas. HTML is a proper subset of SGML.

http

The **h**ypertext **t**ransfer **p**rotocol is the native protocol of browsers and is most typically used to transfer HTML formatted files. The secure version is called "https".

Hurd

The Hurd is the official GNU OS. It is still in development and is not yet supported on too many different processors, but promises to be the most powerful OS available. It (like all the GNU software) is free.

Hz & hertz

Hertz means cycles per second, and makes no assumptions about what is cycling. So, for example, if a fluorescent light flickers once per jiffy, it has a 60 Hz flicker. More typical for computers would be a program that runs once per jiffy and thus has a 60 Hz frequency, or larger units of hertz like kHz, MHz, GHz, or THz.

i18n

Commonly used to abbreviate the word "internationalization". There are eighteen letters between the "i" and the "n". Similar to (and often used along with) i18n.

iCalendar

The iCalendar standard refers to the format used to store calendar type information (including events, to-do items, and journal entries) on the Internet. iCalendar data can be found on some World-Wide-Web pages or attached to e-mail messages.

icon

A small graphical display representing an object, action, or modifier of some sort.

IDE

Loosely speaking, a disk format sometimes used by MS-Windows, Mac OS, AmigaOS, and (rarely) UNIX. EIDE is enhanced IDE; it is much faster. Generally IDE is inferior (but less expensive) to SCSI, but it varies somewhat with system load and the individual IDE and SCSI components themselves. The quick rundown is that: SCSI-I and SCSI-II will almost always outperform IDE; EIDE will almost always outperform SCSI-I and SCSI-II; SCSI-III and UltraSCSI will almost always outperform EIDE; and heavy system loads give an advantage to SCSI. Note that although loosely speaking it is just a format difference, it is deep down a hardware difference.

Inform

A compiled, object-oriented language optimized for creating interactive fiction.

infrared communications

A device with an infrared port can communicate with other devices at a distance by beaming infrared light signals. Two incompatible protocols are used for infrared communications: IrDA and ASK. Many devices support both.

Instant Messenger

AOL's Instant Messenger is is a means of chatting over the Internet in real-time. It allows both open group discussions and private conversations. Instant Messenger uses a different, proprietary protocol from the more standard IRC, and is not supported on as many platforms.

interactive fiction

Interactive fiction (often abbreviated "IF" or "I-F") is a form of literature unique to the computer. While the reader cannot influence the direction of a typical story, the reader plays a more active role in an interactive fiction story and completely controls its direction. Interactive fiction works come in all the sizes and genres available to standard fiction, and in fact are not always even fiction per se (interactive tutorials exist and are slowly becoming more common).

interpreted

If a program is interpreted, its actual human-readable source is read as it is run by the computer. This is generally a slower process than if the program being run has already been compiled.

intranet

An intranet is a private network. There are many intranets scattered all over the world. Some are connected to the Internet via gateways.

IP

IP is the family of protocols that makes up the Internet. The two most common flavors are TCP/IP and UDP/IP.

IRC

Internet relay chat is a means of chatting over the Internet in real-time. It allows both open group discussions and private conversations. IRC programs are provided by many different companies and will work on many different platforms. AOL's Instant Messenger utilizes a separate incompatible protocol but is otherwise very similar.

IrDA

The Infrared Data Association (IrDA) is a voluntary organization of various manufacturers working together to ensure that the infrared communications between different computers, PDAs, printers, digital cameras, remote controls, etc. are all compatible with each other regardless of brand. The term is also often used to designate an IrDA compliant infrared communications port on a device. Informally, a device able to communicate via IrDA compliant infrared is sometimes simply said to "have IrDA". There is also an earlier, incompatible, and usually slower type of infrared communications still in use called ASK.

IRI

An Internationalized Resource Identifier is just a URI with i18n.

IRIX

The variant of UNIX designed by Silicon Graphics, Inc. IRIX machines are known for their graphics capabilities and were initially optimized for multimedia applications.

ISDN

An integrated service digital network line can be simply looked at as a digital phone line. ISDN connections to the Internet can be four times faster than the fastest regular phone connection, and because it is a digital connection a modem is not needed. Any computer hooked up to ISDN will typically require other special equipment in lieu of the modem, however. Also, both phone companies and ISPs charge more for ISDN connections than regular modem connections.

ISP

An Internet service provider is a company that provides Internet support for other entities. AOL (America Online) is a well-known ISP.

Java

A computer language designed to be both fairly lightweight and extremely portable. It is tightly bound to the web as it is the primary language for web applets. There has also been an OS based on Java for use on small hand-held, embedded, and network computers. It is called JavaOS. Java can be either interpreted or compiled. For web applet use it is almost always interpreted. While its interpreted form tends not to be very fast, its compiled form can often rival languages like C++ for speed. It is important to note however that speed is not Java's primary purpose -- raw speed is considered secondary to portabilty and ease of use.

JavaScript

JavaScript (in spite of its name) has nothing whatsoever to do with Java (in fact, it's arguably more like Newton Script than Java). JavaScript is an interpreted language built into a browser to provide a relatively simple means of adding interactivity to web pages. It is only supported on a few different browsers, and tends not to work exactly the same on different versions. Thus its use on the Internet is somewhat restricted to fairly simple programs. On intranets where there are usually fewer browser versions in use, JavaScript has been used to implement much more complex and impressive programs.

jiffy

A jiffy is 1/60 of a second. Jiffies are to seconds as seconds are to minutes.

joystick

A joystick is a physical device typically used to control objects on a computer screen. It is frequently used for games and sometimes used in place of a mouse.

JSON

The JSON is used for data interchange between programs, an area in which the ubiquitous XML is not too well-suited. JSON is lightweight and works extremely cleanly with languages languages including JavaScript, Python, Java, C++, and many others.

JSON-RPC

JSON-RPC is like XML-RPC but is significantly more lightweight since it uses JSON in lieu of XML.

KDE

The **K d**esktop **e**nvironment is a popular free window manager (and much more -- as its name touts, it is more of a desktop environment) that runs under X-Windows.

Kerberos

Kerberos is a network authentication protocol. Basically it preserves the integrity of passwords in any untrusted network (like the Internet). Kerberized applications work hand-in-hand with sites that support Kerberos to ensure that passwords cannot be stolen.

kernel

The very heart of an OS is often called its kernel. It will usually (at minimum) provide some libraries that give programmers access to its various features.

kHz & kilohertz

One kilohertz is equivalent to 1000 hertz. Some older computers have clock speeds measured in kHz.

l10n

Commonly used to abbreviate the word "localization". There are ten letters between the "l" and the "n". Similar to (and often used along with) i18n.

LDAP

The **L**ightweight **D**irectory **A**ccess **P**rotocol provides a means of sharing address book type of information across an intranet or even across the Internet. Note too that "address book type of information" here is pretty broad; it often includes not just human addresses, but machine addresses, printer configurations, and similar.

library

A selection of routines used by programmers to make computers do particular things.

lightweight

Something that is lightweight will not consume computer resources (such as RAM and disk space) too much and will thus run on less expensive computer systems.

Linux

Believe it or not, one of the fastest, most robust, and powerful multitasking OSes is available for free. Linux can be downloaded for free or be purchased on CD-ROM for a small service charge. A handful of companies distribute Linux including Red Hat, Debian, Caldera, and many others. Linux is also possibly available for more hardware combinations than any other OS (with the possible exception of NetBSD. Supported processors include: Alpha, PowerPC, SPARC, x86, and 68xx. Most processors currently not supported are currently works-in-progress or even available in beta. For example, work is currently underway to provide support for PA-RISC, 65xx, StrongARM, and Z80. People have even successfully gotten Linux working on PDAs. As you may have guessed, Linux can be made quite lightweight. Linux is a variant of UNIX and as such, most of the traditional UNIX software will run on Linux. This especially includes the GNU software, most of which comes with the majority of Linux distributions. Fast, reliable, stable, and inexpensive, Linux is popular with ISPs, software developers, and home hobbyists alike.

Lisp

Lisp stands for **list p**rocessing and is the second oldest computer language in the world. Being developed in 1959, it lost the title to FORTRAN by only a few months. It is typically interpreted, but compilers are available for some platforms. Attempts were made to standardize the language, and the standard version is called "Common Lisp". There have also been efforts to simplify the language, and the results of these efforts is another language called Scheme. Lisp is a fairly portable language, but is not particularly fast. Today, Lisp is most widely used with AI software.

load

There are two popular meanings for load. The first means to fetch some data or a program from a disk and store it in memory. The second indicates the amount of work a component (especially a processor) is being made to do.

Logo

Logo is an interpreted language designed by Papert in 1966 to be a tool for helping people (especially kids) learn computer programming concepts. In addition to being used for that purpose, it is often used as a language for controlling mechanical robots and other similar devices. Logo interfaces even exist for building block / toy robot sets. Logo uses a special graphics cursor called "the turtle", and Logo is itself sometimes called "Turtle Graphics". Logo is quite portable but not particularly fast. Versions can be found on almost every computer platform in the world. Additionally, some other languages (notably some Pascal versions) provide Logo-like interfaces for graphics-intensive programming.

lossy

If a process is lossy, it means that a little quality is lost when it is performed. If a format is lossy, it means that putting data into that format (or possibly even manipulating it in that format) will cause some slight loss. Lossy processes and formats are typically used for performance or resource utilization reasons. The opposite of lossy is lossless.

Lua

Lua is a simple interpreted language. It is extremely portable, and free versions exist for most platforms.

Mac OS

Mac OS is the OS used on Macintosh computers. There are two distinctively different versions of it; everything prior to version 10 (sometimes called Mac OS Classic) and everything version 10 or later (called Mac OS X).

Mac OS Classic

The OS created by Apple and originally used by Macs is frequently (albeit slightly incorrectly) referred to as Mac OS Classic (officially Mac OS Classic is this original OS running under the modern Mac OS X in emulation. Mac OS combines the functionality of both an OS and a window manager and is often considered to be the easiest OS to use. It is partially multitasking but will still sometimes crash when dealing with a buggy program. It is probably the second most popular OS, next only to Windows 'XP (although it is quickly losing ground to Mac OS X) and has excellent driver support and boasts a fair selection of games. Mac OS will run on PowerPC and 68xx based machines.

Mac OS X

Mac OS X (originally called Rhapsody) is the industrial strength OS produced by Apple to run on both PowerPC and x86 systems (replacing what is often referred to as Mac OS Classic. Mac OS X is at its heart a variant of UNIX and possesses its underlying power (and the ability to run many of the traditional UNIX tools, including the GNU tools). It also was designed to mimic other OSes on demand via what it originally refered to as "boxes" (actually high-performance emulators); it has the built-in capability to run programs written for older Mac OS (via its "BlueBox", officially called Mac OS Classic) and work was started on making it also run Windows '95 / '98 / ME software (via what was called its "YellowBox"). There are also a few rumors going around that future versions may even be able to run Newton software (via the "GreenBox"). It provides a selection of two window managers built-in: Aqua and X-Windows (with Aqua being the default).

machine language

Machine language consists of the raw numbers that can be directly understood by a particular processor. Each processor's machine language will be different from other processors' machine language. Although called "machine language", it is not usually what people think of when talking about computer languages. Machine language dressed up with mnemonics to make it a bit more human-readable is called assembly language.

Macintosh

A Macintosh (or a Mac for short) is a computer system that has Mac OS for its OS. There are a few different companies that have produced Macs, but by far the largest is Apple. The oldest Macs are based on the 68xx processor; somewhat more recent Macs on the PowerPC processor, and current Macs on the x86 processor. The Macintosh was really the first general purpose computer to employ a GUI.

MacTel

An x86 based system running some flavor of Mac OS.

mainframe

A mainframe is any computer larger than a small piece of furniture. A modern mainframe is more powerful than a modern workstation, but more expensive and more difficult to maintain.

MathML

The **Math M**ark-up **L**anguage is a subset of XML used to represent mathematical formulae and equations. Typically it is found embedded within XHTML documents, although as of this writing not all popular browsers support it.

megahertz

A million cycles per second, abbreviated MHz. This is often used misleadingly to indicate processor speed, because while one might expect that a higher number would indicate a faster processor, that logic only holds true within a given type of processors as different types of processors are capable of doing different amounts of work within a cycle. For a current example, either a 200 MHz PowerPC or a 270 MHz SPARC will outperform a 300 MHz Pentium.

Merced

The Merced is a RISC processor developed by Intel with help from Hewlett-Packard and possibly Sun. It is just starting to be released, but is intended to eventually replace both the x86 and PA-RISC processors. Curiously, HP is recommending that everyone hold off using the first release and instead wait for the second one. It is expected some day to be roughly as fast as an Alpha or PowerPC. It is expected to be supported by future versions of Solaris, Windows-NT, HP-UX, Mac OS X, and Linux. The current semi-available Merced processor is called the Itanium. Its overall schedule is way behind, and some analysts predict that it never will really be released in significant quanities.

MFM

Loosely speaking, An old disk format sometimes used by CP/M, MS-DOS, and MS-Windows. No longer too common as it cannot deliver close to the performance of either SCSI or IDE.

middleware

Software designed to sit in between an OS and applications. Common examples are Java and Tcl/Tk.

MIME

The **m**ulti-purpose **I**nternet **m**ail **e**xtensions specification describes a means of sending non-

ASCII data (such as images, sounds, foreign symbols, etc.) through e-mail. It commonly utilizes bcode.

MMX
Multimedia extensions were built into some x86 CPUs to provide better performance for certain operations, most notably graphics and sound. It is similar to AltiVec on the PowerPC CPUs. Like AltiVec, it requires special software for full performance benefits to be realized.

MOB
A movable object is a graphical object that is manipulated separately from the background. These are seen all the time in computer games. When implemented in hardware, MOBs are sometimes called sprites.

Modula-2 & Modula-3
Modula-2 is a procedural language based on Pascal by its original author in around the 1977 - 1979 time period. Modula-3 is an intended successor that adds support for object-oriented constructs (among other things). Modula-2 can be either compiled or interpreted, while Modula-3 tends to be just a compiled language.

MOTD
A message of the day. Many computers (particularly more capable ones) are configured to display a MOTD when accessed remotely.

Motif
Motif is a popular commercial window manager that runs under X-Windows. Free work-alike versions are also available.

MS-DOS
The DOS produced by Microsoft. Early versions of it bear striking similarities to the earlier CP/M, but it utilizes simpler commands. It provides only a CLI, but either OS/2, Windows 3.1, Windows '95, Windows '98, Windows ME, or GEOS may be run on top of it to provide a GUI. It only runs on x86 based machines.

MS-Windows
MS-Windows is the name collectively given to several somewhat incompatible OSes all produced by Microsoft. They are: Windows CE, Windows NT, Windows 3.1, Windows '95, Windows '98, Windows ME, Windows 2000, and Windows XP.

MUD
A multi-user dimension (also sometimes called multi-user dungeon, but in either case abbreviated to "MUD") is sort of a combination between the online chatting abilities provided by something like IRC and a role-playing game. A MUD built with object oriented principles in mind is called a "Multi-user dimension object-oriented", or MOO. Yet another variant is called a "multi-user shell", or MUSH. Still other variants are called multi-user role-playing environments (MURPE) and multi-user environments (MUSE). There are probably more. In all cases the differences will be mostly academic to the regular user, as the same software is used to connect to all of them. Software to connect to MUDs can be found for most platforms, and there are even Java based ones that can run from within a browser.

multitasking
Some OSes have built into them the ability to do several things at once. This is called multitasking, and has been in use since the late sixties / early seventies. Since this ability is built into the software, the overall system will be slower running two things at once than it will be running just one thing. A system may have more than one processor built into it though, and such a system will be capable of running multiple things at once with less of a performance hit.

nagware
Nagware is a variant of shareware that will frequently remind its users to register.

NetBSD
A free variant of Berkeley UNIX available for Alpha, x86, 68xx, PA-RISC, SPARC, PowerPC, ARM, and many other types of machines. Its emphasis is on portability.

169

netiquette

The established conventions of online politeness are called netiquette. Some conventions vary from site to site or online medium to online medium; others are pretty standard everywhere. Newbies are often unfamiliar with the conventional rules of netiquette and sometimes embarrass themselves accordingly. Be sure not to send that incredibly important e-mail message before reading about netiquette.

newbie

A newbie is a novice to the online world or computers in general.

news

Usenet news can generally be thought of as public e-mail as that is generally the way it behaves. In reality, it is implemented by different software and is often accessed by different programs. Different newsgroups adhere to different topics, and some are "moderated", meaning that humans will try to manually remove off-topic posts, especially spam. Most established newsgroups have a FAQ, and people are strongly encouraged to read the FAQ prior to posting.

Newton

Although Newton is officially the name of the lightweight OS developed by Apple to run on its MessagePad line of PDAs, it is often used to mean the MessagePads (and compatible PDAs) themselves and thus the term "Newton OS" is often used for clarity. The Newton OS is remarkably powerful; it is fully multitasking in spite of the fact that it was designed for small machines. It is optimized for hand-held use, but will readily transfer data to all manner of desktop machines. Historically it was the first PDA. Recently Apple announced that it will discontinue further development of the Newton platform, but will instead work to base future hand-held devices on either Mac OS or Mac OS X with some effort dedicated to making the new devices capable of running current Newton programs.

Newton book

Newton books provide all the functionality of ordinary books but add searching and hypertext capabilities. The format was invented for the Newton to provide a means of making volumes of data portable, and is particularly popular in the medical community as most medical references are available as Newton books and carrying around a one pound Newton is preferable to carrying around twenty pounds of books, especially when it comes to looking up something. In addition to medical books, numerous references, most of the classics, and many contemporary works of fiction are available as Newton books. Most fiction is available for free, most references cost money. Newton books are somewhat more capable than the similar Palm DOC; both are specific types of e-books.

Newton Script

A intepreted, object-oriented language for Newton MessagePad computers.

nybble

A nybble is half a byte, or four bits. It is a case of computer whimsy; it only stands to reason that a small byte should be called a nybble. Some authors spell it with an "i" instead of the "y", but the "y" is the original form.

object-oriented

While the specifics are well beyond the scope of this document, the term "object-oriented" applies to a philosophy of software creation. Often this philosophy is referred to as object-oriented design (sometimes abbreviated as OOD), and programs written with it in mind are referred to as object-oriented programs (often abbreviated OOP). Programming languages designed to help facilitate it are called object-oriented languages (sometimes abbreviated as OOL) and databases built with it in mind are called object-oriented databases (sometimes abbreviated as OODB or less fortunately OOD). The general notion is that an object-oriented approach to creating software starts with modeling the real-world problems trying to be solved in familiar real-world ways, and carries the analogy all the way down to structure of the program. This is of course a great over-simplification. Numerous object-oriented programming languages exist including: Java, C++, Modula-2, Newton Script, and ADA.

Objective-C & ObjC

Objective-C (often called "ObjC" for short) is a compiled object-oriented language. Based heavily on C, Objective-C is nearly as fast and can often be thought of as being just C with added features. Note that it was developed independently of C++; its object-oriented extensions are more in the style of Smalltalk. It is however related to Objective-C++.

Objective-C++ & ObjC++

Objective-C++ (often called "ObjC++" for short) is a curious hybrid of Objective-C and C++, allowing the syntax of both to coexist in the same source files.

office suite

An office suite is a collection of programs including at minimum a word processor, spreadsheet, drawing program, and minimal database program. Some common office suites include MS-Office, AppleWorks, ClarisWorks, GeoWorks, Applixware, Corel Office, and StarOffice.

open source

Open source software goes one step beyond freeware. Not only does it provide the software for free, it provides the original source code used to create the software. Thus, curious users can poke around with it to see how it works, and advanced users can modify it to make it work better for them. By its nature, open souce software is pretty well immune to all types of computer virus.

OpenBSD

A free variant of Berkeley UNIX available for Alpha, x86, 68xx, PA-RISC, SPARC, and PowerPC based machines. Its emphasis is on security.

OpenDocument & ODF

OpenDocument (or ODF for short) is the suite of open, XML-based office suite application formats defined by the OASIS consortium. It defines a platform-neutral, non-proprietary way of storing documents.

OpenGL

A low-level 3D graphics library with an emphasis on speed developed by SGI.

OS/2

OS/2 is the OS designed by IBM to run on x86 based machines. It is semi-compatible with MS-Windows. IBM's more industrial strength OS is called AIX.

PA-RISC

The PA-RISC is a RISC processor developed by Hewlett-Packard. It is currently produced only by HP. At the moment only one OS runs on PA-RISC based machines: HP-UX. There is an effort underway to port Linux to them, though.

Palm DOC

Palm DOC files are quite similar to (but slightly less capable than) Newton books. They were designed for Palm Pilots but can now be read on a couple other platforms, too. They are a specific type of e-book.

Palm Pilot

The Palm Pilot (also called both just Palm and just Pilot, officially now just Palm) is the most popular PDA currently in use. It is one of the least capable PDAs, but it is also one of tho smallest and least expensive. While not as full featured as many of the other PDAs (such as the Newton) it performs what features it does have quite well and still remains truly pocket-sized.

parallel

Loosely speaking, parallel implies a situation where multiple things can be done simultaneously, like having multiple check-out lines each serving people all at once. Parallel connections are by their nature more expensive than serial ones, but usually faster. Also, in a related use of the word, often multitasking computers are said to be capable of running multiple programs in parallel.

partition

Sometimes due to hardware limitations, disks have to be divided into smaller pieces. These pieces are called partitions.

Pascal

Named after the mathematician Blaise Pascal, Pascal is a language designed by Niklaus Wirth originally in 1968 (and heavily revised in 1972) mostly for purposes of education and training people how to write computer programs. It is a typically compiled language but is still usually slower than C or FORTRAN. Wirth also created a more powerful object-oriented Pascal-like language called Modula-2.

PC-DOS

The DOS produced by IBM designed to work like MS-DOS. Early versions of it bear striking similarities to the earlier CP/M, but it utilizes simpler commands. It provides only a CLI, but either Windows 3.1 or GEOS may be run on top of it to provide a GUI. It only runs on x86 based machines.

PCMCIA

The **P**ersonal **C**omputer **M**emory **C**ard **I**nternational **A**ssociation is a standards body that concern themselves with PC Card technology. Often the PC Cards themselves are referred to as "PCMCIA cards". Frequently flash memory can be found in PC card form.

Perl

Perl is an interpreted language extremely popular for web applications.

PET

The Commodore PET (**P**ersonal **E**lectronic **T**ransactor) is an early (circa 1977-1980, around the same time as the Apple][) home computer featuring a ROM-based BASIC developed by Microsoft which it uses as a default "OS". It is based on the 65xx family of processors and is the precursor to the VIC-20.

PETSCII

The PETSCII character set gets its name from "**PET** ASCII; it is a variant of the ASCII character set originally developed for the Commodore PET that swaps the upper and lower case characters and adds over a hundred graphic characters in addition to other small changes. If you encounter some text that seems to have uppercase where lowercase is expected and vice-versa, it is probably a PETSCII file.

PHP

Named with a recursive acronym (PHP: Hypertext Preprocessor), PHP provides a means of creating web pages that dynamically modify themselves on the fly.

ping

Ping is a protocol designed to check across a network to see if a particular computer is "alive" or not. Computers that recognize the ping will report back their status. Computers that are down will not report back anything at all.

pixel

The smallest distinct point on a computer display is called a pixel.

plug-in

A plug-in is a piece of software designed not to run on its own but rather work in cooperation with a separate application to increase that application's abilities.

point

There are two common meanings for this word. The first is in the geometric sense; a position in space without size. Of course as applied to computers it must take up some space in practise (even if not in theory) and it is thus sometimes synonomous with pixel. The other meaning is related most typically to fonts and regards size. The exact meaning of it in this sense will unfortunately vary somewhat from person to person, but will often mean 1/72 of an inch. Even when it does not exactly mean 1/72 of an inch, larger point sizes always indicate larger fonts.

PowerPC

The PowerPC is a RISC processor developed in a collaborative effort between IBM, Apple, and Motorola. It is currently produced by a few different companies, of course including its original developers. A few different OSes run on PowerPC based machines, including Mac OS, AIX, Solaris, Windows NT, Linux, Mac OS X, BeOS, and AmigaOS. At any given time, the fastest processor in the world is usually either a PowerPC or an Alpha, but sometimes SPARCs and PA-RISCs make the list, too.

proprietary
This simply means to be supplied by only one vendor. It is commonly misused. Currently, most processors are non-proprietary, some systems are non-proprietary, and every OS (except for arguably Linux) is proprietary.

protocol
A protocol is a means of communication used between computers. As long as both computers recognize the same protocol, they can communicate without too much difficulty over the same network or even via a simple direct modem connection regardless whether or not they are themselves of the same type. This means that WinTel boxes, Macs, Amigas, UNIX machines, etc., can all talk with one another provided they agree on a common protocol first.

Psion
The Psion is a fairly popular brand of PDA. Generally, it is in between a Palm and a Newton in capability. It runs the EPOC OS.

Python
Python is an interpreted, object-oriented language popular for Internet applications. It is extremely portable with free versions existing for virtually every platform.

queue
A queue is a waiting list of things to be processed. Many computers provide printing queues, for example. If something is being printed and the user requests that another item be printed, the second item will sit in the printer queue until the first item finishes printing at which point it will be removed from the queue and get printed itself.

QuickDraw
A high-level 3D graphics library with an emphasis on quick development time created by Apple.

RAM
Random access memory is the short-term memory of a computer. Any information stored in RAM will be lost if power goes out, but the computer can read from RAM far more quickly than from a drive.

random access
Also called "dynamic access" this indicates that data can be selected without having to skip over earlier data first. This is the way that a CD, record, laserdisc, or DVD will behave -- it is easy to selectively play a particular track without having to fast forward through earlier tracks. The other common behavior is called sequential access.

RDF
The Resource Description Framework is built upon an XML base and provides a more modern means of accessing data from Internet resources. It can provide metadata (including annotations) for web pages making (among other things) searching more capable. It is also being used to refashion some existing formats like RSS and iCalendar; in the former case it is already in place (at least for newer RSS versions), but it is still experimental in the latter case.

real-time
Something that happens in real-time will keep up with the events around it and never give any sort of "please wait" message.

Rexx
The Restructured Extended Executor is an interpreted language designed primarily to be embedded in other applications in order to make them consistently programmable, but also to be easy to learn and understand.

RISC
Reduced instruction set computing is one of the two main types of processor design in use

today, the other being CISC. The fastest processors in the world today are all RISC designs. There are several popular RISC processors, including Alphas, ARMs, PA-RISCs, PowerPCs, and SPARCs.

robot
A robot (or 'bot for short) in the computer sense is a program designed to automate some task, often just sending messages or collecting information. A spider is a type of robot designed to traverse the web performing some task (usually collecting data).

robust
The adjective robust is used to describe programs that are better designed, have fewer bugs, and are less likely to crash.

ROM
Read-only memory is similar to RAM only cannot be altered and does not lose its contents when power is removed.

RSS
RSS stands for either Rich Site Summary, Really Simple Syndication, or RDF Site Summary, depending upon whom you ask. The general idea is that it can provide brief summaries of articles that appear in full on a web site. It is well-formed XML, and newer versions are even more specifically well-formed RDF.

Ruby
Ruby is an interpreted, object-oriented language. Ruby was fairly heavily influenced by Perl, so people familiar with that language can typically transition to Ruby easily.

scanner
A scanner is a piece of hardware that will examine a picture and produce a computer file that represents what it sees. A digital camera is a related device. Each has its own limitations.

Scheme
Scheme is a typically interpreted computer language. It was created in 1975 in an attempt to make Lisp simpler and more consistent. Scheme is a fairly portable language, but is not particularly fast.

script
A script is a series of OS commands. The term "batch file" means much the same thing, but is a bit dated. Typically the same sort of situations in which one would say DOS instead of OS, it would also be appropriate to say batch file instead of script. Scripts can be run like programs, but tend to perform simpler tasks. When a script is run, it is always interpreted.

SCSI
Loosely speaking, a disk format sometimes used by MS-Windows, Mac OS, AmigaOS, and (almost always) UNIX. Generally SCSI is superior (but more expensive) to IDE, but it varies somewhat with system load and the individual SCSI and IDE components themselves. The quick rundown is that: SCSI-I and SCSI-II will almost always outperform IDE; EIDE will almost always outperform SCSI-I and SCSI-II; SCSI-III and UltraSCSI will almost always outperform EIDE; and heavy system loads give an advantage to SCSI. Note that although loosely speaking it is just a format difference, it is deep down a hardware difference.

sequential access
This indicates that data cannot be selected without having to skip over earlier data first. This is the way that a cassette or video tape will behave. The other common behavior is called random access.

serial
Loosely speaking, serial implies something that has to be done linearly, one at a time, like people being served in a single check-out line. Serial connections are by their nature less expensive than parallel connections (including things like SCSI) but are typically slower.

server
A server is a computer designed to provide various services for an entire network. It is typically

either a workstation or a mainframe because it will usually be expected to handle far greater loads than ordinary desktop systems. The load placed on servers also necessitates that they utilize robust OSes, as a crash on a system that is currently being used by many people is far worse than a crash on a system that is only being used by one person.

SGML
The Standard Generalized Mark-up Language provides an extremely generalized level of mark-up. More common mark-up languages like HTML and XML are actually just popular subsets of SGML.

shareware
Shareware is software made for profit that allows a trial period before purchase. Typically shareware can be freely downloaded, used for a period of weeks (or sometimes even months), and either purchased or discarded after it has been learned whether or not it will satisfy the user's needs.

shell
A CLI designed to simplify complex OS commands. Some OSes (like AmigaOS, the Hurd, and UNIX) have built-in support to make the concurrent use of multiple shells easy. Common shells include the Korn Shell (ksh), the Bourne Shell (sh or bsh), the Bourne-Again Shell, (bash or bsh), the C-Shell (csh), etc.

SIMM
A physical component used to add RAM to a computer. Similar to, but incompatible with, DIMMs.

Smalltalk
Smalltalk is an efficient language for writing computer programs. Historically it is one of the first object-oriented languages, and is not only used today in its pure form but shows its influence in other languages like Objective-C.

Solaris
Solaris is the commercial variant of UNIX currently produced by Sun. It is an industrial strength, nigh bulletproof, powerful multitasking OS that will run on SPARC, x86, and PowerPC based machines.

spam
Generally spam is unwanted, unrequested e-mail or Usenet news. It is typically sent out in bulk to huge address lists that were automatically generated by various robots endlessly searching the Internet and newsgroups for things that resemble e-mail addresses. The legality of spam is a topic of much debate; it is at best only borderline legal, and spammers have been successfully persecuted in some states.

SPARC
The SPARC is a RISC processor developed by Sun. The design was more or less released to the world, and it is currently produced by around a dozen different companies too numerous to even bother mentioning. It is worth noting that even computers made by Sun typically sport SPARCs made by other companies. A couple different OSes run on SPARC based machines, including Solaris, SunOS, and Linux. Some of the newer SPARC models are called UltraSPARCs.

sprite
The term sprite originally referred to a small MOB, usually implemented in hardware. Lately it is also being used to refer to a single image used piecemeal within a Web site in order to avoid incurring the time penalty of downloading multiple files.

SQL
SQL (pronounced Sequel) is an interpreted language specially designed for database access. It is supported by virtually every major modern database system.

Sugar
The window manager used by the OLPC XO. It is made to run on top of Linux.

28

SunOS

SunOS is the commercial variant of UNIX formerly produced (but still supported) by Sun.

SVG

Scalable Vector Graphics data is an XML file that is used to hold graphical data that can be resized without loss of quality. SVG data can be kept in its own file, or even embedded within a web page (although not all browsers are capable of displaying such data).

Tcl/Tk

The Tool Command Language is a portable interpreted computer language designed to be easy to use. Tk is a GUI toolkit for Tcl. Tcl is a fairly popular language for both integrating existing applications and for creating Web applets (note that applets written in Tcl are often called Tcklets). Tcl/Tk is available for free for most platforms, and plug-ins are available to enable many browsers to play Tcklets.

TCP/IP

TCP/IP is a protocol for computer networks. The Internet is largely built on top of TCP/IP (it is the more reliable of the two primary Internet Protocols -- TCP stands for Transmission Control Protocol).

terminator

A terminator is a dedicated device used to mark the end of a device chain (as is most typically found with SCSI devices). If such a chain is not properly terminated, weird results can occur.

TEX

TEX (pronounced "tek") is a freely available, industrial strength typesetting program that can be run on many different platforms. These qualities make it exceptionally popular in schools, and frequently software developed at a university will have its documentation in TEX format. TEX is not limited to educational use, though; many professional books were typeset with TEX. TEX's primary drawback is that it can be quite difficult to set up initially.

THz & terahertz

One terahertz is equivalent to 1000 gigahertz.

TrackBack

TrackBacks essentially provide a means whereby different web sites can post messages to one another not just to inform each other about citations, but also to alert one another of related resources. Typically, a blog may display quotations from another blog through the use of TrackBacks.

UDP/IP

UDP/IP is a protocol for computer networks. It is the faster of the two primary Internet Protocols. UDP stands for User Datagram Protocol.

Unicode

The Unicode character set is a superset of the ASCII character set with provisions made for handling international symbols and characters from other languages. Unicode is sixteen bit, so takes up roughly twice the space as simple ASCII, but is correspondingly more flexible.

UNIX

UNIX is a family of OSes, each being made by a different company or organization but all offering a very similar look and feel. It can not quite be considered non-proprietary, however, as the differences between different vendor's versions can be significant (it is still generally possible to switch from one vendor's UNIX to another without too much effort; today the differences between different UNIXes are similar to the differences between the different MS-Windows; historically there were two different UNIX camps, Berkeley / BSD and AT&T / System V, but the assorted vendors have worked together to minimalize the differences). The free variant Linux is one of the closest things to a current, non-proprietary OS; its development is controlled by a non-profit organization and its distribution is provided by several companies. UNIX is powerful; it is fully multitasking and can do pretty much anything that any OS can do (look to the Hurd if you need a more powerful OS). With power comes complexity, however, and

29

UNIX tends not to be overly friendly to beginners (although those who think UNIX is difficult or cryptic apparently have not used CP/M). Window managers are available for UNIX (running under X-Windows) and once properly configured common operations will be almost as simple on a UNIX machine as on a Mac. Out of all the OSes in current use, UNIX has the greatest range of hardware support. It will run on machines built around many different processors. Lightweight versions of UNIX have been made to run on PDAs, and in the other direction, full featured versions make full advantage of all the resources on large, multi-processor machines. Some different UNIX versions include Solaris, Linux, IRIX, AIX, SunOS, FreeBSD, Digital UNIX, HP-UX, NetBSD, OpenBSD, etc.

upload
To upload a file is to copy it from your computer to a remote computer. The opposite is download.

UPS
An uninterrupted power supply uses heavy duty batteries to help smooth out its input power source.

URI
A Uniform Resource Identifier is basically just a unique address for almost any type of resource. It is similar to but more general than a URL; in fact, it may also be a URN.

URL
A Uniform Resource Locator is basically just an address for a file that can be given to a browser. It starts with a protocol type (such as http, ftp, or gopher) and is followed by a colon, machine name, and file name in UNIX style. Optionally an octothorpe character "#" and and arguments will follow the file name; this can be used to further define position within a page and perform a few other tricks. Similar to but less general than a URI.

URN
A Uniform Resource Name is basically just a unique address for almost any type of resource unlike a URL it will probably not resolve with a browser.

USB
A really fast type of serial port that offers many of the best features of SCSI without the price. Faster than many types of parallel port, a single USB port is capable of chaining many devices without the need of a terminator. USB is much slower (but somewhat less expensive) than FireWire.

uucode
The point of uucode is to allow 8-bit binary data to be transferred through the more common 7-bit ASCII channels (most especially e-mail). The facilities for dealing with uucoded files exist for many different machine types, and the most common programs are called "uuencode" for encoding the original binary file into a 7-bit file and "uudecode" for restoring the original binary file from the encoded one. Sometimes different uuencode and uudecode programs will work in subtly different manners causing annoying compatibility problems. Bcode was invented to provide the same service as uucode but to maintain a tighter standard.

variable width
As applied to a font, variable width means that different characters will have different widths as appropriate. For example, an "i" will take up much less space than an "m". The opposite of variable width is fixed width. The terms "proportional width" and "proportionally spaced" mean the same thing as variable width. Some common variable width fonts include Times, Helvetica, and Bookman.

VAX
The VAX is a computer platform developed by Digital. Its plural is VAXen. VAXen are large expensive machines that were once quite popular in large businesses; today modern UNIX workstations have all the capability of VAXen but take up much less space. Their OS is called VMS.

vector

This term has two common meanings. The first is in the geometric sense: a vector defines a direction and magnitude. The second concerns the formatting of fonts and images. If a font is a vector font or an image is a vector image, it is defined as lines of relative size and direction rather than as collections of pixels (the method used in bitmapped fonts and images). This makes it easier to change the size of the font or image, but puts a bigger load on the device that has to display the font or image. The term "outline font" means the same thing as vector font.

Veronica & Veronica2

Although traditionally written as a proper name, Veronica is actually an acronym for "**very easy rodent-oriented netwide index to computerized archives**", where the "rodent" refers to gopher. The acronym was obviously a little forced to go along with the pre-existing (and now largely unused) Archie, in order to have a little fun with a comic book reference. Regardless, Veronica (or these days more likely Veronica2) is essentially a search engine for gopher resources.

VIC-20

The Commodore VIC-20 computer sold millions of units and is generally considered to have been the first affordable home computer. It features a ROM-based BASIC and uses it as a default "OS". It is based on the 65xx family of processors. VIC (in case you are wondering) can stand for either **v**ideo **i**nterface **c** or **v**ideo **i**nterface **c**omputer. The VIC-20 is the precursor to the C64/128.

virtual machine

A virtual machine is a machine completely defined and implemented in software rather than hardware. It is often referred to as a "runtime environment"; code compiled for such a machine is typically called bytecode.

virtual memory

This is a scheme by which disk space is made to substitute for the more expensive RAM space. Using it will often enable a comptuer to do things it could not do without it, but it will also often result in an overall slowing down of the system. The concept of swap space is very similar.

virtual reality

Virtual reality (often called VR for short) is generally speaking an attempt to provide more natural, human interfaces to software. It can be as simple as a pseudo 3D interface or as elaborate as an isolated room in which the computer can control the user's senses of vision, hearing, and even smell and touch.

virus

A virus is a program that will seek to duplicate itself in memory and on disks, but in a subtle way that will not immediately be noticed. A computer on the same network as an infected computer or that uses an infected disk (even a floppy) or that downloads and runs an infected program can itself become infected. A virus can only spread to computers of the same platform. For example, on a network consisting of a WinTel box, a Mac, and a Linux box, if one machine acquires a virus the other two will probably still be safe. Note also that different platforms have different general levels of resistance; UNIX machines are almost immune, Win '95 / '98 / ME / XP is quite vulnerable, and most others lie somewhere in between.

VMS

The industrial strength OS that runs on VAXen.

VoIP

VoIP means "Voice over IP" and it is quite simply a way of utilizing the Internet (or even in some cases intranets) for telephone conversations. The primary motivations for doing so are cost and convenience as VoIP is significantly less expensive than typical telephone long distance packages, plus one high speed Internet connection can serve for multiple phone lines.

VRML

A **V**irtual **R**eality **M**odeling **L**anguage file is used to represent VR objects. It has essentially been superceded by X3D.

W3C
The World Wide Web Consortium (usually abbreviated W3C) is a non-profit, advisory body that makes suggestions on the future direction of the World Wide Web, HTML, CSS, and browsers.

Waba
An extremely lightweight subset of Java optimized for use on PDAs.

WebDAV
WebDAV stands for Web-based Distributed Authoring and Versioning, and is designed to provide a way of editing Web-based resources in place. It serves as a more modern (and often more secure) replacement for FTP in many cases.

WebTV
A WebTV box hooks up to an ordinary television set and displays web pages. It will not display them as well as a dedicated computer.

window manager
A window manager is a program that acts as a graphical go-between for a user and an OS. It provides a GUI for the OS. Some OSes incorporate the window manager into their own internal code, but many do not for reasons of efficiency. Some OSes partially make the division. Some common true window managers include CDE (Common Desktop Environment), GNOME, KDE, Aqua, OpenWindows, Motif, FVWM, Sugar, and Enlightenment. Some common hybrid window managers with OS extensions include Windows ME, Windows 98, Windows 95, Windows 3.1, OS/2 and GEOS.

Windows '95
Windows '95 is currently the second most popular variant of MS-Windows. It was designed to be the replacement Windows 3.1 but has not yet done so completely partly because of suspected security problems but even more because it is not as lightweight and will not work on all the machines that Windows 3.1 will. It is more capable than Windows 3.1 though and now has excellent driver support and more games available for it than any other platform. It is made to run on top of MS-DOS and will not do much of anything if MS-DOS is not on the system. It is thus not strictly an OS per se, but nor is it a true window manager either; rather the combination of MS-DOS and Windows '95 result in a full OS with GUI. It is partially multitasking but has a much greater chance of crashing than Windows NT does (or probably even Mac OS) if faced with a buggy program. Windows '95 runs only on x86 based machines. Currently Windows '95 has several Y2K issues, some of which have patches that can be downloaded for free, and some of which do not yet have fixes at all.

Windows '98
Windows '98 is quite possibly the second most popular form of MS-Windows, in spite of the fact that its official release is currently a point of legal debate with at least nineteen states, the federal government, and a handful of foreign countries as it has a few questionable features that might restrict the novice computer user and/or unfairly compete with other computer companies. It also has some specific issues with the version of Java that comes prepackaged with it that has never been adequately fixed, and it still has several Y2K issues, most of which have patches that can be downloaded for free (in fact, Microsoft guarantees that it will work properly through 2000 with the proper patches), but some of which do not yet have fixes at all (it won't work properly through 2001 at this point). In any case, it was designed to replace Windows '95.

Windows 2000
Windows 2000 was the intended replacement for Windows NT and in that capacity received relatively lukewarm support. Being based on Windows NT, it inherits some of its driver support problems. Originally it was also supposed to replace Windows '98, but Windows ME was made to do that instead, and the merger between Windows NT and Windows '98 was postponed until Windows XP.

Windows 3.1
Windows 3.1 remains a surprisingly popular variant of MS-Windows. It is lighter weight than

either Windows '95 or Windows NT (but not lighter weight than GEOS) but less capable than the other two. It is made to run on top of MS-DOS and will not do much of anything if MS-DOS is not on the system. It is thus not strictly an OS per se, but nor is it a true window manager, either; rather the combination of MS-DOS and Windows 3.1 result in a full OS with GUI. Its driver support is good, but its game selection is limited. Windows 3.1 runs only on x86 based machines. It has some severe Y2K issues that may or may not be fixed.

Windows CE

Windows CE is the lightweight variant of MS-Windows. It offers the general look and feel of Windows '95 but is targetted primarily for hand-held devices, PDAs, NCs, and embedded devices. It does not have all the features of either Windows '95 or Windows NT and is very different from Windows 3.1. In particular, it will not run any software made for any of the other versions of MS-Windows. Special versions of each program must be made. Furthermore, there are actually a few slightly different variants of Windows CE, and no variant is guaranteed to be able to run software made specifically for another one. Driver support is also fairly poor for all types, and few games are made for it. Windows CE will run on a few different processor types, including the x86 and several different processors dedicated to PDAs, embedded systems, and hand-held devices.

Windows ME

Windows ME is yet another flavor of MS-Windows (specifically the planned replacement for Windows '98). Windows ME currently runs only on the x86 processor.

Windows NT

Windows NT is the industrial-strength variant of MS-Windows. Current revisions offer the look and feel of Windows '95 and older revisions offer the look and feel of Windows 3.1. It is the most robust flavor of MS-Windows and is fully multitasking. It is also by far the most expensive flavor of MS-Windows and has far less software available for it than Windows '95 or '98. In particular, do not expect to play many games on a Windows NT machine, and expect some difficulty in obtaining good drivers. Windows NT will run on a few different processor types, including the x86, the Alpha, and the PowerPC. Plans are in place to port Windows NT to the Merced when it becomes available.

Windows Vista

Windows Vista is the newest flavor of MS-Windows (specifically the planned replacement for Windows XP). Windows Vista (originally known as Longhorn) currently only runs on x86 processors.

Windows XP

Windows XP is yet another flavor of MS-Windows (specifically the planned replacement for both Windows ME and Windows 2000). Windows XP currently only runs on the x86 processors. Windows XP is currently the most popular form of MS-Windows.

WinTel

An x86 based system running some flavor of MS-Windows.

workstation

Depending upon whom you ask, a workstation is either an industrial strength desktop computer or its own category above the desktops. Workstations typically have some flavor of UNIX for their OS, but there has been a recent trend to call high-end Windows NT and Windows 2000 machines workstations, too.

WYSIWYG

What you see is what you get; an adjective applied to a program that attempts to exactly represent printed output on the screen. Related to WYSIWYM but quite different.

WYSIWYM

What you see is what you mean; an adjective applied to a program that does not attempt to exactly represent printed output on the screen, but rather defines how things are used and so will adapt to different paper sizes, etc. Related to WYSIWYG but quite different.

X-Face

X-Faces are small monochrome images embedded in headers for both provides a e-mail and news messages. Better mail and news applications will display them (sometimes automatically, sometimes only per request).

X-Windows

X-Windows provides a GUI for most UNIX systems, but can also be found as an add-on library for other computers. Numerous window managers run on top of it. It is often just called "X".

X3D

Extensible 3D Graphics data is an XML file that is used to hold three-dimensional graphical data. It is the successor to VRML.

x86

The x86 series of processors includes the Pentium, Pentium Pro, Pentium II, Pentium III, Celeron, and Athlon as well as the 786, 686, 586, 486, 386, 286, 8086, 8088, etc. It is an exceptionally popular design (by far the most popular CISC series) in spite of the fact that even its fastest model is significantly slower than the assorted RISC processors. Many different OSes run on machines built around x86 processors, including MS-DOS, Windows 3.1, Windows '95, Windows '98, Windows ME, Windows NT, Windows 2000, Windows CE, Windows XP, GEOS, Linux, Solaris, OpenBSD, NetBSD, FreeBSD, Mac OS X, OS/2, BeOS, CP/M, etc. A couple different companies produce x86 processors, but the bulk of them are produced by Intel. It is expected that this processor will eventually be completely replaced by the Merced, but the Merced development schedule is somewhat behind. Also, it should be noted that the Pentium III processor has stirred some controversy by including a "fingerprint" that will enable individual computer usage of web pages etc. to be accurately tracked.

XBL

An XML Binding Language document is used to associate executable content with an XML tag. It is itself an XML file, and is used most frequently (although not exclusively) in conjunction with XUL.

XHTML

The Extensible Hypertext Mark-up Language is essentially a cleaner, stricter version of HTML. It is a proper subset of XML.

XML

The Extensible Mark-up Language is a subset of SGML and a superset of XHTML. It is used for numerous things including (among many others) RSS and RDF.

XML-RPC

XML-RPC provides a fairly lightweight means by which one computer can execute a program on a co-operating machine across a network like the Internet. It is based on XML and is used for everything from fetching stock quotes to checking weather forcasts.

XO

The energy-efficient, kid-friendly laptop produced by the OLPC project. It runs Sugar for its window manager and Linux for its OS. It sports numerous built-in features like wireless networking, a video camera & microphone, a few USB ports, and audio in/out jacks. It comes with several educational applications (which it refers to as "Activities"), most of which are written in Python.

XSL

The Extensible Stylesheet Language is like CSS for XML. It provides a means of describing how an XML resource should be displayed.

XSLT

XSL Transformations are used to transform one type of XML into another. It is a component of XSL that can be (and often is) used independently.

XUL

An XML User-Interface Language document is used to define a user interface for an application using XML to specify the individual controls as well as the overall layout.

Y2K

The general class of problems resulting from the wrapping of computers' internal date timers is given this label in honor of the most obvious occurrence -- when the year changes from 1999 to 2000 (abbreviated in some programs as 99 to 00 indicating a backwards time movement). Contrary to popular belief, these problems will not all manifest themselves on the first day of 2000, but will in fact happen over a range of dates extending out beyond 2075. A computer that does not have problems prior to the beginning of 2001 is considered "Y2K compliant", and a computer that does not have problems within the next ten years or so is considered for all practical purposes to be "Y2K clean". Whether or not a given computer is "clean" depends upon both its OS and its applications (and in some unfortunate cases, its hardware). The quick rundown on common home / small business machines (roughly from best to worst) is that:

All Mac OS systems are okay until at least the year 2040. By that time a patch should be available.

All BeOS systems are okay until the year 2040 (2038?). By that time a patch should be available.

Most UNIX versions are either okay or currently have free fixes available (and typically would not have major problems until 2038 or later in any case).

NewtonOS has a problem with the year 2010, but has a free fix available.

Newer AmigaOS systems are okay; older ones have a problem with the year 2000 but have a free fix available. They also have a year 2077 problem that does not yet have a free fix.

Some OS/2 systems have a year 2000 problem, but free fixes are available.

All CP/M versions have a year 2000 problem, but free fixes are available.

PC-DOS has a year 2000 problem, but a free fix is available.

DR-DOS has a year 2000 problem, but a free fix is available.

Different versions of GEOS have different problems ranging from minor year 2000 problems (with fixes in the works) to larger year 2080 problems (that do not have fixes yet). The only problem that may not have a fix in time is the year 2000 problem on the Apple][version of GEOS; not only was that version discontinued, unlike the other GEOS versions it no longer has a parent company to take care of it.

All MS-Windows versions (except possibly Windows 2000 and Windows ME) have multiple problems with the year 2000 and/or 2001, most of which have free fixes but some of which still lack free fixes as of this writing. Even new machines off the shelf that are labelled "Y2K Compliant" usually are not unless additional software is purchased and installed. Basically WinNT and WinCE can be properly patched, Windows '98 can be patched to work properly through 2000 (possibly not 2001), Windows '95 can be at least partially patched for 2000 (but not 2001) but is not being guaranteed by Microsoft, and Windows 3.1 cannot be fully patched.

MS-DOS has problems with at least the year 2000 (and probably more). None of its problems have been addressed as of this writing. Possible fixes are to change over to either PC-DOS or DR-DOS.

Results vary wildly for common applications, so it is better to be safe than sorry and check out the ones that you use. It should also be noted that some of the biggest expected Y2K problems will be at the two ends of the computer spectrum with older legacy mainframes (such as power some large banks) and some of the various tiny embedded computers (such as power most burglar alarms and many assorted appliances). Finally, it should also be mentioned that some older WinTel boxes and Amigas may have Y2K problems in their hardware requiring a card addition or replacement.

Z-Machine

A virtual machine optimized for running interactive fiction, interactive tutorials, and other interactive things of a primarily textual nature. Z-Machines have been ported to almost every platform in use today. Z-machine bytecode is usually called Z-code. The Glulx virtual machine is of the same idea but somewhat more modern in concept.

Z80

The Z80 series of processors is a CISC design and is not being used in too many new stand-alone computer systems, but can still be occasionally found in embedded systems. It is the most popular processor for CP/M machines.

Zaurus

The Zaurus is a brand of PDA. It is generally in between a Palm and a Newton in capability.

zip

There are three common zips in the computer world that are completely different from one another. One is a type of removable removable disk slightly larger (physically) and vastly larger (capacity) than a floppy. The second is a group of programs used for running interactive fiction. The third is a group of programs used for compression.

Zoomer

The Zoomer is a type of PDA. Zoomers all use GEOS for their OS and are / were produced by numerous different companies and are thus found under numerous different names. The "classic" Zoomers are known as the Z-7000, the Z-PDA, and the GRiDpad and were made by Casio, Tandy, and AST respectively. Newer Zoomers include HP's OmniGo models, Hyundai's Gulliver (which may not have actually been released to the general public), and Nokia's Communicator line of PDA / cell phone hybrids.

———